The Trials of a Co

Augustus Jessopp

Alpha Editions

This edition published in 2024

ISBN : 9789362095992

Design and Setting By
Alpha Editions
www.alphaedis.com
Email - info@alphaedis.com

Contents

PREFACE.

IN a volume which I published three years ago1 I attempted to give a faithful picture of the habits and ways of thinking, the superstitions, prejudices and grounds for discontent, the grievances and the trials, of the country folk among whom my lot was cast and among whom it was my duty and my privilege to live as a country clergyman. I was surprised, and not a little pained, to hear from many who read my book that the impression produced upon them was exactly the reverse of that which I had desired to convey. On returning to a country village after long residence in a large town, I found things greatly changed, of course; but I found that, though the country folk had not shared in the general progress which had been going on in the condition of the urban population, they still retained some of their sturdy virtues, still had some love for their homes, still clung to some of their old prejudices which reflected their attachment to their birthplace, and that if they were inclined to surrender themselves to the leadership of blatant demagogues, and to dwell upon some real or imagined wrongs coarsely exaggerated by itinerant agitators with their living to get by speechifying, it was not because there was no cause for discontent. The rustics were right when they followed their instincts and these told them that their lot might be easily—so very easily—made much happier than it is, if philanthropists would only give themselves a fair chance, set themselves patiently to study facts before committing themselves to crude theories, try to make themselves really conversant with the conditions which they vaguely desire to ameliorate, go to work in the right way and learn to take things by the right handles.

The circumstances under which I commenced residence in my country parish were, unhappily, not conducive to my forming a favourable judgment of my people. I was at starting brought face to face with the worst side of their characters. They were and had for long been in bad hands; they had surrendered themselves to the guidance of those who had gone very far towards demoralizing them. I could not be blind to the faults—the vices if you will—which were only too apparent. I could not but grieve at the altered *tone* which was observable in their language and their manners, since the days when I had been a country curate twenty years before. But while I lamented the noticeable deterioration and the fact that the rustics were less cordial, less courteous, less generous, less loving, and, therefore, less happy than they had been, I gradually got to see that the surface may be ruffled and yet the inner nature beneath that surface may have some depths unaffected by the turmoil. The charity which hopeth all things suggested that it was the time to work and wait. It was not long before I learnt to feel something more than mere interest in my people. I learnt to love them. I learnt—

To see a good in evil, and a hope
In ill success; to sympathize, be proud
Of their half-reasons, faint aspirings, dim
Struggles for truth, their poorest fallacies,
Their prejudice, and fears, and cares, and doubts,
Which all touch upon nobleness, despite
Their error, all tend upwardly though weak,
Like plants in mines which never see the sun,
But dream of him, and guess where he may be,
And do their best to climb and get at him.

I was shocked when friendly critics told me I had drawn a melancholy picture, and that to live in such a community, and with surroundings such as I had described, must be depressing, almost degrading, for any man of culture and refinement.

The essays which follow in this volume were written as a kind of protest against any such view of the case. I think the two volumes—this and my former one—should in fairness be read each as the complement of the other. In "Arcady" I have drawn, as best I could, the picture of the life of the rustics around me. In this volume I have sketched the life of a country parson trying to do his best to elevate those among whom he has been called to exercise his ministry.

I hold that any clergyman in a country parish who aims *exclusively* at being a Religious Teacher will miss his aim. He must be more, or he will fail to be that. He must be a social power in his parish, and he ought to try, at any rate, to be an intellectual force also. It is because I am strongly convinced of this that I have brought so much into prominence the daily intercourse which I have enjoyed with my people on the footing of a mere friendly neighbour. I cannot think that I have any right at all to lift the veil from those private communings with penitents who are agonized by ghastly memories, with poor weaklings torturing themselves with religious difficulties, or at the bedside of the sick and dying. These seem to me to be most sacred confidences which we are bound to conceal from others as if they had been entrusted to us under a sacramental obligation of impenetrable silence. We all have our share of miserable experiences of this kind. We have no right to talk of them; they never can become common property without some one alive or dead being betrayed. In the single instance in which I may seem to have departed from this principle, it was the expressed wish of the poor woman whose sad story I told that others should learn the circumstances of the case which I made public.

It may be thought, perhaps, that my surroundings have something peculiar in them. But, No! they are of the ordinary type. For two centuries or so East Anglia was indeed greatly cut off from union and sympathy with the rest of England, and was a kingdom apart. The result has been that there are certain characteristics which distinguish the Norfolk character, and some of them are not pleasing. These are survivals, and they present some difficulties to him who is not an East Anglian born, when he is first brought face to face with them. But in the main we are all pretty much alike, and let a man be placed where he may, he will be sure to find something new in the situation, and almost as sure to make some mistakes at starting. I do not believe that a man of average ability, who is really in earnest in his desire to do the best he can for his people, and who throws himself heartily into his work, will find one place worse than another. Let him resolve to find his joy in the performance of his duty according to his light, and the joy will come. So far from repining at my own lot, I have found it—I do find it—a very happy one; and if I have dwelt on the country parson's trials, I have done so in no petty and querulous spirit as if I had anything to complain of which others had not—this I should disdain to do—but rather as protesting that they press upon my brethren equally as upon myself, and that, such as they are, some must be, some need not be, some ought not to be.

As for the worries and annoyances, the "trials" which are inseparable from our position, it is the part of a wise man to make the best of them, and to put as good a face upon them as he can. But with regard to such matters as ought not to be and need not be, it behoves us all to look about us to discover if possible some remedy for the remediable, to find out the root and source of any evil which is a real evil, to lift up our voices against an abuse which has grown or is growing to be intolerable, and by no means to acquiesce in the continuance of that which is obviously working to the serious prejudice of the community. While every other class is crying out for Reform and getting it by simply raising the cry, it is a reproach upon us clergy—and I fear we deserve the reproach—that we are a great deal too ready to submit to the continuance of scandals and abuses rather than face the risks which *any* change is likely to bring upon our order. In no other profession is a man more certain to be regarded as a dangerous character, wanting in loyalty and wanting in humility, who is even suspected of a desire to improve upon the arrangements which have existed since time was young, or of advocating measures which would interfere with the order of procedure that was good enough for our grandfathers, and therefore must be good enough for ourselves. It really seems to be the belief of some among us that our Constitution in Church or State never *grew* at all, but *chrystalized* into its present form, and dropped from heaven in perfect panoply like Minerva from the head of Jove. To point a finger at the texture of the awful *peplos*, and to hint that it was woven in the looms of this world, is to bring upon oneself the charge of impiety. And yet these men are wrong. Organic bodies grow because they are alive; when theycease to grow and are no longer capable of adapting themselves to the changes that are going on around them, they die. Nothing can prolong their life. If you cramp and fetter a living thing by swathing it round about with iron bands that may force it to keep exactly the form it presented a thousand years ago—then you will kill it. It is only a question of time when your slaying process will prove successful. As for the other method of "letting things slide," that is, if possible, more foolish than the other, and certainly more cowardly. What can be baser than the craven whine, "It will last our time"? An institution which has lasted through a long line of centuries, and which will *only* last our time, may be approaching dissolution from lack of inherent vitality, but it may also be in peril because of the despairing supineness of its pledged defenders.

I have lifted up my voice against one relic of the past which is most certainly doomed because it has been allowed to exist a great deal too long already; it is a *survival* which I am deeply convinced is answerable for much of the corruption that hurts us, much of the offence taken and given, much of the laxity and very much of the deplorable want of discipline existing among us.

The legal status of the beneficed clergy, in virtue of which they are freeholders for life in their several benefices, does not quite stand alone. The Parish Clerk, too, has a freehold in his benefice, and, after formal admission to it, he may retain it without fear of being turned out of it as long as the breath remains in his body. These freeholds in an office have been swept away in every other department of the public service, though they died hard and cost a good deal to abolish. The buying and selling of "places" and reversions or next presentations to them was as common in the State as in the Church not so very long ago. The odious system was swept away for ever by the simple expedient of making every public servant removable at pleasure for negligence, misconduct, inefficiency, or even less. It is only among the holders of ecclesiastical preferment that the old abomination survives. Because it survives, other things survive too which ought not to be tolerated. The first and foremost of these is the open sale of the right to present a clerk in orders to a cure of souls. But that is the least mischievous consequence of the present system being retained. There are other consequences which are far more serious. Among them is the almost entire want of movement and change, in the lives of the country clergy; the absence of fresh interests and of the invigorating stimulus of a new career, however humble, with new associations to give a zest to the performance, it may be, of the old duties, but discharged now among those who do not know all that you have to say, and are not yet tired of the sound of your voice, or at any rate thinking they would like to hear another. The rule in our country parishes is that where a man is set down at first, there he dies at last. Exchange of benefices is, I admit, more common than it used to be, partly because the benefices themselves are less valuable and less jealously kept in the patrons' hands than they were; but even now exchanges are not often made and are not "negotiated" without some difficulty. To begin with, before two clergymen can change their cures, however much they may themselves be agreed, it is necessary that the consent of two patrons and two bishops should be obtained as a preliminary; and this is not always to be got for the asking. If a patron has bestowed preferment upon a clergyman with whose ministrations he is contented and something more, he is not too willing to part with him. If he has been so unfortunate as to have given the living to the wrong man, there may be very good reasons why he should not choose to be a party to such a transaction as would result in passing on a clerical scamp or incompetent from one cure to another. But in any case it by no means follows that, because I have presented a parson to a cure of souls, I should therefore give him the next presentation too, if he happens to be tired of his cure and anxious to go elsewhere. The result is that, as a rule, a beneficed clergyman, when once he finds himself, irremovable, in his cure, gives up all thought of leaving it. It is "a certainty," and gradually he gets to look for nothing better; he goes through his duties as best he can, however mournfully conscious that he has lost the old fire and force and efficiency; he takes comfort in the thought that he has worked his parish while he could, and that he is entitled to take it easily now; and, indeed, in the eyes of those about him, he grows more and more picturesque and venerable, just as the old church tower does—but it is not safe to ring the bells up there when so much restoration is wanted.

I have dealt with this subject in some detail in the Fourth Paper in this volume. At the time it appeared, the public mind was much occupied with and disturbed by certain political questions then in the ascendant, and the essay fell dead, attracted little or no attention and, in fact, was read by few. It often happens that a book proves an utter failure by being published at the wrong time—a month too soon or a month too late. The favour of the reading public is very capricious, not always awarded to the most deserving, sometimes given with a kind of fury of acclamation to a lucky literary adventurer whose reputation "rushes up like the rocket and comes down like the stick." Moreover the essay laboured under one rather serious defect, which I have not yet set myself to remedy by appending an almost necessary supplement. For it may be asked, and it has indeed been objected, "If every beneficed clergyman were to hold his appointment subject to removal, ought not some provision to be made for his retirement in old age or when physically or mentally unfit for the discharge of his sacred functions?" Yes! By all means. But why only the *beneficed* clergy? Why not all who are admitted to the sacred office? Surely it would not be difficult to elaborate a scheme whereby every officiating clergyman should be compelled to make provision for his family, or for his own retirement, by the simple expedient of stopping a certain percentage of his income and investing it in his name—much in the same way that the Clive fund is managed in India, or as the compulsory insurance of railway servants is enforced by some of the great companies. Until something of this sort is carried out, we shall continue to be pained by those distressing appeals for clergymen's families reduced to beggary by the death of the bread-winner, which come to us all with increasing frequency, and which, as matters now look, are not likely to be fewer in the near future.

This however, is only a part, and I venture to think not quite a vital part, of the other question, which as a great national question appears to me of much greater importance. That question may be put in very few words. Is it for the advantage of the Church or the nation that the incomes of the clergy should continue to be assured to them by a different tenure from that which prevails in the case of all other public servants—a tenure which in the latter case was proved to be working prejudicially to the interests of the community at large, and which it was found absolutely necessary to abolish?

It is easy to raise a cry against any one who dares to ask such a question as this by denouncing him as an Erastian. But our clerical *incomes* are one thing, our sacred functions and office are another. All the Parliaments in the world can never admit me or any one else to Holy Orders: but there is nothing to prevent a rich man from endowing any church or chapel with an income to be enjoyed by the parson of that church only under certain conditions or for a certain limited time. People seem to think that it is of the very essence of an endowment that the income derived from it should belong to the man who is once admitted to enjoy it as long as he lives and chooses to draw the pay. If by anything I have written, or could write, I could exercise any influence in the direction of leading thoughtful men to give their serious attention to this subject and to discuss it earnestly, I should have very little doubt about the result, and I should feel that I had not lived in vain.

Very closely allied with this question is another which is forcing itself upon us all with increasing urgency every month. When we begin to ask ourselves and one another to whom do our Village Churches belong? Who is bound to keep them from falling into ruin? Who has the right to sell the lead off the roof, or the books in the ancient Parish Library, or the bells in the steeple, or the very brasses in the pavement?—and all these things have been done and nobody been called to account—when, I say, we begin to ask these things and press for an answer, we may well be dismayed by the suspicion of how anomalous our position is. The Society for the Preservation of Ancient Buildings has been doing good work for us; it deserves more support than it has received, and needs many more subscribers before its influence can be brought to bear upon the ignorance and Vandalism, and right down rascality too, with which it so often finds itself in conflict. But the work of this society, *as things are*, can never be anything but palliative at the utmost. A local Philistine with a long purse and no more conscience or sentiment than a gorilla, may do almost what he pleases. It is dreadful to think what might be perpetrated in our country churches with impunity, and what *would be* perpetrated too, if only the true state of the case were known. Here, too, there is need for the reform of the law. Who *do* the churches belong to? Who are responsible for their protection from outrage and destruction? There are some country parishes where with a very little manipulation the inhabitants in Vestry assembled might be induced to vote anything; even to the using superfluous seats for boarding up all the windows on the north side to make themselves snug withal. What is to prevent their doing it? Who is to bell the cat?

The Fifth Paper in this volume may not at first sight appear to have anything to do with a Country Parson's "trials"; and yet it has. There are some people who are never tired of declaiming against the uselessness of our Cathedral buildings. More than once I have been put upon the defensive when railers have lifted up their voices especially against the waste of space which might be turned to good account in our own glorious East Anglian Cathedral. When they whose chief amusement in life it is to find fault are on the look out for something to rail at, they will never be without an excuse for indulging in their amiable pastime. That there are many spaces which might, with great advantage, be made available for worthy purposes in most of our cathedrals, must be apparent to any one who thinks about the matter. The question is, what are worthy purposes, and how may those vacant spaces be best turned to account without sacrificing the dignity of those majestic buildings and their surroundings, and without vulgarising them by introducing associations out of harmony with the traditions that belong to them and, the sentiment of reverence that they arouse? Who that has seen the Cathedral Library at Ely, could doubt whether it is in the right place or no? Or who that knows anything of what has been doing of late among the Archives of Canterbury or Lincoln, can help wishing that such work were doing elsewhere? But why should not our cathedrals become the great storehouses for all our ancient muniments, in which they might find the protection they deserve and the intelligent supervision which might render them accessible to students of our history?

Little need be said to justify the appearance of the Sixth Paper in a volume which professes to treat of a Country Parson's "trials." I hope I have made it appear that even such a trial as this is bearable—nay! that it is one of those which may even become a very delightful trial indeed to those who have some resources in themselves, and whose occupations and tastes are such as to make them habitually regret that the winter days are so short, and sometimes even half complain because the summer sunshine brings such irresistible temptations to be idle.

Is it true that we poor country parsons have our trials? Then do not grudge us such comfort as we can find in being snowed up in Arcady.

The last Essay in the volume may be taken as a hint that among other trials which a Country Parson has to bear is the necessity of acquiescing in certain unsatisfied yearnings. That sounds so very heroic now that I have written it, that I am inclined to be rather proud of my own resignation. All my life I have had a hankering to pay a visit to the United States of America. There was a time when I could have afforded the expense of such a trip, but I could not then afford to give the time. Now with an annually decreasing income the *way* is open, but the *means* are not forthcoming. But as I think of too many of my brethren who every day of their lives are sadly put to it to keep the wolf from the door and find it difficult to provide even the bare necessaries of life, not to speak of those comforts and simple indulgences which it is so hard to miss when old age and its infirmities have set in—the contrast between their lot and my own comes home to me almost with a sense of self-reproach. Let them whose sterner trials are so much more hard to bear than mine, forgive the irony of one who grumbles that he is too poor to cross the Atlantic on a new voyage of discovery—

as though that were a serious deprivation and a proof of his being only one step from indigence. Let them do him the justice to believe that he himself is not insensible to the pathos that lurks in the background of his own lament.

I.
THE TRIALS OF A COUNTRY PARSON.

MY friends from Babylon the great are very good to me in the summer-time. They come in a delightful stream from their thousand luxuries, their great social gatherings, their brilliant talk, and their cheering and stimulating surroundings; they come from all the excitement and the whirl of London or some other huge city where men *live*, and they make their friendly sojourn with us here in the wilderness even for a week at a time. They come in a generous and self-denying spirit to console and condole with the man whom they pity so gracefully—the poor country parson "relegated," as Bishop Stubbs is pleased to express it, "to the comparative uselessness of literary (and clerical) retirement." I observe that the first question my good friends ask is invariably this: "What shall we do and where shall we go—to-morrow?" It would be absurd to suppose that any man in his senses comes to the wilderness to *stay* there, or that there could be anything to *do* there. A man goes to a place to see, not the place itself, but some other place. When you find yourself in the wilderness you may use any spot in it as a point of departure, but as a dwelling-place, a resting-place, never!

Moreover, I observe that, by the help of such means of locomotion as we have at command, the days pass merrily enough with my visitors in fine weather. But as sure as ever the rain comes, so surely do my friends receive important letters calling them back, much to their distress and disappointment. If the weather be *very* bad—obstinately bad—or if a horse falls lame and cannot be replaced, or some equally crushing disaster keeps us all confined to the house and garden, my visitors invariably receive a telegram which summons them home instantly even at the cost of having to send for a fly to the nearest market town. Sometimes, by a rare coincidence, a kindly being drops in upon us even in the winter. He is always genial, cordial, and a great refreshment, but he never stays a second night. We keep him warm, we allow a liberal use of "the shameful," we give him meat and drink of the best, we flatter him, we coddle him, we talk and draw him out, we "show him things," but he never stays over that single night; and when he goes, as he shakes our hands and wraps himself up in his rugs and furs, I notice that he has a sort of *conflate* expression upon his countenance; his face is as a hybrid flower where two beauties blend. One eye says plainly, "I *am* a lucky dog, for I am going away at last," and the other eye, beaming with kindliness, sometimes with affection, says just as plainly, "Poor old boy, how I do pity you!"

Well! this is a pitiful age; that is, it is an age very full of pity. The ingenuity shown by some good people in finding out new objects of commiseration is truly admirable. It is hardly to be expected that the country parson should escape the general appetite for shedding tears over real or supposed sufferers.

But it strikes some of us poor forlorn ones as not a little curious that our grand town friends never by any chance seem to see what there is in our lot that is really pathetic or trying. "How often do you give it meat?" said a blushing, mild-eyed, lank-haired young worthy in my hearing the other day. "Lawk! sir, that don't have no meat," answered the laughing mother, as she hugged her tiny baby closer to her bosom. "Never have meat? How dreadful!" Just so! But it is not only ludicrous, it is annoying, to be pitied for the wrong thing; and though I am not inclined to maintain the thesis that we, the soldiers of God's army of occupation, who are doing outpost duty, pass our lives in a whirl of tumultuous and delicious joy, yet, if I am to be pitied, do let me be pitied intelligently. I cannot expect to be envied, but surely it is not such a very heavy calamity for a man never to catch a sight of *Truth* or *The World*, or to find that there is not such a thing as an oyster-knife in his parish.

Moreover, side by side with pity, there is a large amount of much more irritating and ignorant exaggeration of the good things we are supposed to enjoy. We do not, I admit, hear quite so often as formerly about "fat livings" and "valuable preferment," nor about the "rectorial mansion with a thousand a year"; but we hear a great deal more about such fabulous lands of Goshen than we ought to hear. There is always a disposition to represent our neighbours as better off than ourselves, and whereas the salaried townsman knows that his income, whatever it may be, is his net income which he may count upon as his spending fund to use as *he* pleases, when he hears of others as receiving or entitled to receive so many pounds a year, he assumes that they do receive it and that they may spend it as *they* please. The townsman, again, who moves among the multitude and every hour is reminded of that multitude pressing, as all fluids do, "equally in all directions," hears, and sometimes he knows, that the clergy in the towns have immense claims upon their time and are always on the move in the streets and courts. They are always about, always *en évidence*. If a man has only to minister to a paltry seven hundred, what *can* he have to do? He must be a drone.

Moreover, the aforesaid townsman has read all about those country parsons. You can hardly take up a novel without finding a sleek rector figuring in the volumes. These idealized rural clerics always remind me of Mr. Whistler's *Nocturnes*. The figures roll at you through the mists that are gathering round them. The good people who try to introduce us to these reverend characters very rarely venture upon a firm and distinct outline. The truth is, that for the most part the novelists never slept in a country parsonage in their lives, never knew a country parson out of a book.

A year or two ago my friend X. was dining in a London mansion. "Who's that?" said a lady opposite, as she ducked her head in his direction and looked at her partner. X. turned to speak to *his* partner, but could not help hearing the scarcely whispered dialogue: "A country parson, did you say? Why, he's tall!"

And their voices low with fashion, not with feeling, softly freighted
All the air about the windows with elastic laughter sweet.

It was quite a surprise to that lady novelist that a country parson could be tall! Many men are tall—policemen, for instance. But only short men ought to be country parsons. Why! we shall hear of one of them being good-looking next!

When any class of men feel themselves to be the butt of others, they are apt to be a little cowed. They hold their peace and fret, and if they resent their hard treatment and speak out, they rarely do themselves justice. Very few men can come well out of a *snub*, and the countryman who is not used to it never knows what to reply to offensive language. Yet worms have been known to turn, not that I ever heard they got any good by it; they can't bite, and they can't sting, but I suppose it comforts them to deliver their own souls. Poor worms! Yes! you may pity them.

*   *   *   *   *

But if the country parson has his trials, how may he hope to be listened to when he desires to make it clear what they are? Where shall he begin? Where shall he begin if not by pointing to that delicate nerve-centre of draped humanity, exquisite in its sensitiveness, knowing no rest in its perpetual giving out of force, for ever hungering for renewal of its exhausted resources, feeling no pain in its plethora and dreading no death save from inanition—to wit, the Pocket? Touch a man's pocket, and a shudder thrills through every fibre.

The country parson has a great deal to complain of at the hands of those who will persist in talking of him as an exceptionally thriving stipendiary. It is one thing to say that in all cases he gets more than he deserves; it is quite another to put forth unblushingly that his income is half as much again as in fact it is, and his outgoings only what the outgoings of other men are. Logicians class the *suppressio veri* among sophisms; but would it not be better to call that artful proceeding a fraud? "Drink fair, Betsy, whatever you do!" said Mrs. Gamp on a memorable occasion. Yes, if it is only out of the teapot.

i. With regard to the income of the country parson, it may be laid down as a fact not to be disputed, that hardly one per cent. of the country clergy ever *touch* the full amount which theoretically they are entitled to receive. In the case of parishes where the land is much subdivided, and where there are a number of small tithepayers, it would be almost impossible for the clergyman personally to collect his dues; he almost invariably employs an agent, who is not a likely man to do his work for love. Even the agent can rarely get in all the small sums that the small folk ought to pay. Even he has to submit to occasional defalcations, and to consider whether it is worth while to press the legal rights of his employer too far. Moreover, the small folk from time immemorial have expected something in the shape of a tithe dinner or a tithe tea, for which the diners or the tea-drinkers do not pay, you may be sure; this constitutes a not inconsiderable abatement on the sum-total of receipts which ought to come to hand at the tithe audit.

Taking one year with another, it may be accepted as a moderate estimate that the cost of collecting his tithe, *plus* bad debts in some shape or other, amounts to six per cent., and he who gets within seven per cent. of his clerical income gets more than most of us do. But the law allows of no abatement in respect of this initial charge; and because the law takes up this ground, the world at large assumes that the nominal gross income of the benefice does come into the pockets of the incumbent. The world at large is quite certain that nobody in his senses makes a return of a *larger* income than he enjoys, and if the parson pays on £500, people assume that he does not get *less* from his living than that. The world at large does not know that the parson is not asked to make a return. The surveyor makes up his books on the tithe commutation table for the parish, and on that the parson is assessed, whatever he may say.

ii. For be it known it is with the surveyor or rate-collector that the parson's first and most important concern lies. Whatever he may receive from his cure, however numerous may be the defaulters among the tithe-payers, however large the expense of collecting his dues, the parson has *to pay rates* on his gross income. The barrister and the physician, the artist or the head of a government department, knows or need know nothing about rates. He may live in a garret if he likes; he may live in a boarding-house at so much a week; he may live in a flat at a rent which covers all extraneous charges. I suppose we most of us have known men of considerable fortune, men who live in chambers, men who live in lodgings, men who live in college rooms, who never *directly* paid a rate in their lives. Our lamented H., who dropped out recently, leaving £97,000 behind him, invested in first-class securities, was one of these languidly prosperous men. "I do detetht violent language on any thubject whatever," he lisped out to me once. "I hope I thall never thee that man again who thtormed at rate collectorth tho. What *ith* a rate collector? Doth he wear a uniform?"

But a country parson and all that he has in the world, *qua* country parson, is rateable to his very last farthing, and beyond it: the fiction being that he is a landed proprietor, and as such in the enjoyment of an income from real property. It is in vain that he pleads that his nominal income is of all property the most unreal:—he is told that he has a claim upon the land, and the land cannot run away. It is in vain that he plaintively protests that he would gladly live in a smaller house if he were allowed—he *does* live in it, chained to it like a dangerous dog to his kennel. It is in vain that he urges that he cannot let his glebe, and may not cut down the trees upon it—that he is compelled to keep his house in tenantable repair, and maintain the fences as he found them. The impassive functionary expresses a well-feigned regret and some guarded commiseration; but he has his duty to perform, and the rates have to be paid—Poor rates, County rates, School Board rates, and all the rest of them; and paid upon that parson's gross income—such an income as never comes, and which everybody knows never could be collected.

You may say in your graceful way that a parson does not pay a bit more than he ought to pay, and that he may be thankful if he be allowed to live at all. That may be quite true—I don't think it is, but it *may be*—but there are some things that are not true, and one of them is, that the gross income awarded to the country parson on paper gives anything approaching to a fair notion of the amount of income that comes to his hands. And if you are going to pity the country parson, do begin at the right end, and consider how you would like to pay such rates as he pays on *your* gross income.

iii. But when the country parson's rates have been duly paid, the next thing that he is answerable for is the Land-tax. The mysteries of the Land-tax are quite beyond me. If I could afford to give up three years of my life to the uninterrupted study of the history and incidence of the Land-tax, I think, by what people tell me, I might get to know something about it, and be in a position to enlighten mankind upon this abstruse subject; but as I really have not three years of my life to spare, I must needs acquiesce in my hopeless ignorance even to the end. Only this I do know, that, whereas the country parson is called upon to pay sixpence in the pound for Income-tax, he is called upon to pay nearly ninepence in the pound for Land-tax: at any rate, I know one country parson who has to do so.

Let the Land-tax pass—it is beyond me. But how about the Income-tax? As I have said above, in the case of all other professions except the clerical, a man makes his return of income upon the *available* income which comes to him after deducting all fair and reasonable *office expenses*. But for the crime of clericalism, the country parson is debarred from making any such deductions as are permitted to other human beings. Many of the "good livings" in East Anglia have two churches, each of which must be served. A man cannot be in two places at once; and the laws of nature and of the Church being in conflict, the laws of the Church carry it over the laws of nature, and the rector has to put in an appearance at his second church by deputy—in other words, the poor man has to keep a curate. If he were a country solicitor who was compelled to keep a clerk, he would deduct the salary of the clerk from the profits of his business; but being only a country parson, he can do nothing of the sort: he has to pay Income-tax all the same on his gross returns. A curate is a luxury, as a riding horse is a luxury; and the only wonder is that curates have not long ago been included among those superfluous animals chargeable to the assessed taxes.

iv. Perhaps the most irritating of all imposts that press upon the country parson is that to which he has to submit because the churchyard is technically part of his freehold. In many parts of the country a fee is charged for burying the dead. In the diocese of Norwich there are no burial fees. The right of burying his dead in the churchyard is a right which may be claimed by any inhabitant of the parish; the soil of the churchyard is said to belong to the parishioners; the *surface of the soil* belongs to the parson. This being so, the parson is assessed in the books of the parish for the assumed value of the herbage growing upon the soil, and on this assumed value he is accordingly compelled to pay rates, Income-tax, and Land-tax. Of course the parson could legally turn cattle or donkeys into the churchyard to disport themselves among the graves; but happily that man who should venture to do this nowadays would be thought guilty of an outrage upon all decency. Who of us is there who does not rejoice that this state of feeling has grown up among us? But the result is that the churchyard, so far from being a source of income to the parson, has become a source of expense to him in almost all cases. Somebody has to keep the grass mown, and see that God's acre is not desecrated. Few of us grumble at that; and some who have large resources pride themselves on keeping their churchyards as a lawn is kept or a garden. But it surely is monstrous when everybody knows that the churchyard, so far from bringing the parson any pecuniary benefit, entails an annual expense upon him which is practically unavoidable—it is monstrous, I say, that the parson should be assessed upon the value of the crop which might be raised off dead men's graves, and that he should be taxed for showing an example of decency and right feeling to those around him.

"Well! But why don't you appeal?"

My excellent sir, do you suppose that nobody ever has appealed? Do you suppose that very original idea of yours has never occurred to any one else before? Or do you suppose that we the shepherds of Arcady, find appealing against an assessment, made by our neighbours to relieve themselves, before the magistrates at Quarter Sessions, is a process peculiarly pleasurable and particularly profitable when the costs are defrayed? We grumble or fret, we count it among our trials, but we say, "After all, it is only about five shillings a-year. Anything for a quiet life. Let it go!" So the wrong gets to be established as a right. But it is none the less a wrong because it continues to exist, or because in coin of the realm it amounts to a trifle. Was it Mr. Midshipman Easy's nurse who urged in excuse of her moral turpitude in having an infant of her very own, "Please, ma'am, it was *such* a little one?"

The grievance of having to pay rates on the churchyard may be in one sense a little one. But when it comes to being charged rates upon the premiums you pay upon your insurance policies, some of them—the insurance of his church and other buildings—being compulsory payments, and upon the mortgage of your benefice effected in your predecessor's time—even the sneerer at a sentimental grievance could hardly call such charges as these not worth making a fuss about. In many a needy country parson's household the rates make all the difference whether his children can have butter to their bread or not.

*   *   *   *   *

It must be obvious to most people from what has been already said—and much more might be said—that, unless a country parson have some resources outside of any income derivable from his benefice, he must needs be a very poor man. Our people know this better than any one else, and it is often a very anxious question on the appointment of a new incumbent whether he will live in the same style as that which his predecessor maintained. Will he keep a carriage, or only a pony chaise? Will he employ two men in the garden? Will he "put out his washing?"2 Will his house be a small local market for poultry and butter and eggs? Will he farm the glebe or let it? How many servants will he keep, and will the lady want a girl to train in the kitchen or the nursery from time to time? Such questions as these are sometimes very anxious ones in a remote country village where every pound spent among the inhabitants serves to build up a *margin* outside the ordinary income of the wage-earners, and which helps the small occupiers to tide over many a temporary embarrassment when money is scarce, and small payments have to be met and cannot any longer be deferred.

Let me, before going any further, deal with a question which I have had suggested to me again and again by certain peculiar people with dearly beloved theories of their own. It is often asked, Ought clergymen ever to be rich men? Is not a rich clergyman out of place in a country parsonage? Does not his wealth raise him too far above the level of his people? Does it not make him sit loosely to his duties? Does not the fact of a country parson being known to be a rich man tend *to demoralize* a parish?

Lest it should be supposed that the present writer is one of the fortunate ones rolling in riches, and therefore in a manner bound to stand up for his own class—let it be at once understood that the present writer is a man of straw, one of those men to whom the month of January is a month of deep anxiety, perplexity, and depression of soul. Yet he would disdain to join the band of whining grumblers only because one year after another he finds that he must content himself with the corned beef and carrots, and cannot by hook or by crook afford to indulge in some very desirable recreation or expense which the majority of his acquaintance habitually regard as absolutely necessary if existence is to be endured at all. No! I am very far indeed from being a rich man; but this I am bound to testify in common fairness to my wealthier brethren in the ministry of the Church of England, that if any impartial person, with adequate knowledge of the facts, were asked to point out the most devoted, zealous, unworldly, and practically efficient country parsons in the diocese of Norwich—for let me speak as I do know—he would without hesitation name first and foremost some of the richest of the clergy in the eastern counties.

Do you desire that your son should begin his ministerial life under a man of great ability, sound sense, courage, and religious earnestness, a man who never spares himself and will not suffer his subordinates to sink into slovenly frivolity and idleness, then make your approaches to Lucullus, and you will have cause to thank God if the young fellow serves his apprenticeship under a guide and teacher such as this. He will learn no nonsense there, and see no masquerading, only an undemonstrative but unflinching adherence to the path believed to be the path of duty, and a manliness of self-surrender such as can only arouse an enthusiasm of respect and esteem.

Does "our own correspondent" wish to see how a score of infamous hovels can be changed into a score of model cottages which pay interest on the cost of their erection, and which in half a dozen years have helped perceptibly to raise the tone and tastes and habits of the population till it really looks as if some barbarians could be civilized by a *coup de main?*—let him pay a visit to the parish of our Reverend Hercules, only one of whose many labours it has been to cleanse an Augean stable. It will do him good to see the mighty shoulders of that rugged philanthropist, him of the broad brow and the great heart and the deep purse, always at work and always at home, about the very last man in England to be suspected of belonging to the sickly sort of puling visionaries.

Do you want to meet with a type of the saintly parish priest, one after holy George Herbert's heart, one with hardly a thought that does not turn upon the service of the sanctuary or the duties that he owes to his scattered flock? Come with me, and we will go together and look at one of the most beautiful village churches in the land, on which our devout Ambrose has spent his thousands only with deep gratitude that he has been permitted to spend them so—and with never a word of brag or publicity, never a paragraph foisted into the newspapers. And as we pass out of that quiet churchyard, trim as a queen's parterre, I will show you the window of that little study which Ambrose has not thought it right to enlarge, and if he be not there, be sure we shall find him at his school or by the sick-bed of the poor, or inquiring into some case of sorrow or sin where a kindly hand or a wise word may peradventure solace the sad or go some way to raise the fallen.

What country parson among all the nine hundred and odd within this unwieldy diocese has lived a simpler or more devoted life than our Nestor—[Greek: γέρων ἱππηλάτα Νέστωρ]—he who for more than threescore years and ten has gone in and out among his people, and doing his pastoral work so naturally, so much as a matter of course, that no one thinks of his being a rich man, except when those towering horses of his stop at our lowly portals and have to be corkscrewed into our diminutive stables?

And who knows not of thee, Euerges, treasurer and secretary and general mainstay of every good work, the idol of thy people and their healer, the terror of the impostor, and the true friend of all that deserve thy helping hand and purse! or thee, too, Amomos, who after thirty years of work as an evangelist in the city, spending there thyself and thy substance all the while, hast now betaken thee to the poor villagers, if haply some little good may yet be done among the lowly ones before the night cometh when no man can work?

"But do not such well-meaning gentlemen as these *demoralize* the poor?" Oh dear yes! of course they do. It is so very demoralizing to help a lame dog over a stile. It does so pauperize a broken-down couple to whom the Poor Law Guardians allow three shillings a week and half a stone of flour, if you give them a sack of potatoes about Christmas time. It corrupts and degrades Biddy Bundle to bestow an old petticoat upon her when she is shivering with the cold, and it takes all self-respect and independence from the unruly bosom of Dick the fiddler to offer him your old hat or a shabby pair of trousers. The truest, wisest, most far-sighted and most magnanimous charity is to let Harry Dobbs have "an order for the house" when he is out of work and short of coals—Harry Dobbs, who set himself against all the laws of political economy, and married at eighteen, when he had not the wherewithal to buy the chairs and tables. So we country parsons are a demoralizing force in the body politic forsooth, because we cannot bear to see poor people starve at our gates. We have been known actually to give soup to a reckless couple guilty of twelve children; actually soup! And we have dropped corrupting shillings into trembling hands, only because they were trembling, and distributed ounces of tobacco to the inmates of the Union, and poisoned the souls of old beldames with gratuitous half-pounds of tea. And we counsel people to come to church, when they would much rather go to the public-house, and we coddle them and warm them now and then, and instead of leaving them to learn manliness and independence and self-reliance on twelve shillings a week, we step between them and the consequences of their own improvidence, and we disturb the action of the beautiful laws of the universe, and where we see the ponderous wheels of Juggernaut just going to roll over a helpless imbecile who has tripped and dropped, we must needs make a clutch at him and pull him out by the scruff of the neck, and tell him to get up

and not do it again. And all this is *demoralizing* and *pauperizing,*
is it?

Out upon you! you miserable prigs with your chatter and
babble! *You* to talk of the parson's narrowness and his bigotry
and his cant? *You* to sneer at him for being the slave of a
superstition? *You* to pose as the only thinkers with all the logic
of all the philosophers on your side, all the logic and never a
crumb of common sense to back it? Bigotry and intolerance
and cant and class jealousy and scorn—that refuge for the
intellectually destitute and the blustering coward—where will
you find them in all their most bitter and sour and hateful
intensity, if not among the new lights, the self-styled
economists? And we have to sit mum and let brainless
pretenders superciliously put us out of court with a self-
complacent wave of the hand, as they give utterance to perky
platitudes about the clergy pauperizing the working man. No,
Mr. Dandy Dryskull. No! this gospel of yours, a little trying to
listen to, is being found out; ours will see the end of it.

You preach Sir Andrew and his love of law,And we the
Saviour and His law of love!

I, for one, hereby proclaim and declare that I intend to help
the sick and aged and struggling poor whenever I have the
chance, and as far as I have the means, and I hope the day will
never come when I shall cease to think without shame of him
who is said to have made it his boast that he had never given a
beggar a penny in his life. I am free to confess that I draw the
line somewhere. I do draw the line at the tramp—I do find it
necessary to be uncompromising there. Indeed I keep a big dog
for the tramp, and that dog, inasmuch as he passes his happy
life in a country parsonage—that dog, I say, is *not* muzzled.

"But don't you get imposed upon? Don't you get asked to
replace dead horses and cows and pigs and donkeys, that never
walked on four legs and no mortal eye ever saw in the land of
the living?"

Of course we do! Is it a prerogative of the country parson to
be duped by a swindler? Oh, Mr. Worldly Wiseman, were you
never taken in? Never! Then, sir, I could not have you for a
son-in-law! As for us—we country parsons—we do
occasionally get imposed upon in very absurd and
contemptible fashion. Sometimes we submit to be bled with
our eyes open. A bungling bumpkin has managed to get his

horse's leg broken by his own stupidity. We know that the fellow was jiggling the poor brute's teeth out of his mouth at the time, or the animal would never have shown himself as great an idiot as his master. But there stands the master horseless, with the tears in his eyes, and we know all about him and the hard struggle he has had to keep things going, and we say to ourselves, "I wonder what would happen to *me* if my horse dropped down dead some fine morning. Who would help *me* to another? and what then?" So we pull out the sovereign, and give the fellow a note to somebody else, and that is how we demoralize *him*.

Or another comes at night-time and wants to speak to us on very particular business, and implores us to tide him over a real difficulty, and.... "What? do you mean to say, you lend fellows money?" Yes. I mean to say I have even done that and very very rarely repented of it, and I mean to say there are men, and women too, to whom I would lend money again if I had it; but it does not follow that I would lend it to everybody, least of all that I would lend it to you, Mr. Worldly Wiseman. Try it on, sir! Try it on! and see whether you would depart triumphant from the interview!

Moreover, the country parson has always to pay a little—just a very little—more than any one else for most things that come to his door. The market has always risen when he wants to buy, and has always suddenly fallen when he wants to sell. The small man's oats are invariably superior to any one's when he has a small parcel to dispose of to the parson. As to the price of hay, when the parson has to buy it, that is truly startling. I never see half a rood of carrots growing in a labourer's allotment, but I feel sure I shall have to buy those carrots before Christmas, and sorry as I am to observe how rarely any fruit trees are ever planted in a poor man's garden, I reflect that perhaps it is just as well, for already the damsons and the apples that besiege the rectory are almost overwhelming. I never ask what becomes of them, but it is morally and physically impossible that they should be eaten under this roof. "But, my dear, you must buy Widow Coe's damsons; nobody else will, you know!" This is what I am told is "considering the poor people"; that is our way of putting it. You, Mr. Worldly Wiseman, you call it demoralizing them.

Then, too, the country parson is expected to "encourage the local industries." I wonder whether they make pillow-lace in

Bedfordshire as they did once. If they do, and especially if the demand for it in the outer world has waned, the country parsons' wives in that part of England must have a very trying time of it.

Once, when I was in the merry twenties, a dirty old hag with an evil report, but no worse than other people, except that she was an old slut, knocked at my back door and asked to see "The Lady Shepherd." Mrs. Triplet was a Mormonite, at any rate her husband was; and it was credibly believed that Mrs. Triplet herself had been baptized by immersion in a horsepond in the dead of night, dressed as Godiva was dressed during her famous ride, and seated, not upon a palfrey, but upon a jackass. How Triplet could ever have been converted to a belief in polygamy with his experience of the married state, I am entirely unable to explain. But Mrs. Triplet came to our door and asked for "The Lady Shepherd." It was a delicate piece of flattery. She must have thought over it a long time. Was not the parson the shepherd? a bad one it might be, a hireling, a blind leader of the blind, but still a shepherd. Then his wife must needs be a shepherdess—and she did not look like it—or a sheep—No! that wouldn't do at all—or the shepherd's lady—and shepherds don't have ladies; or—happy thought!—the Lady Shepherd.

Accordingly Mrs. Triplet asked for the Lady Shepherd. Mrs. Triplet in former times had been a tailor's hand, and in that capacity had made a few shillings a week by odd jobs for the Cambridge tailors in term time; but she had married, and now she lived too far away in the wilds to be able to continue at her old employment, and being a bad manager, she soon had to cast about for some new source of income. In the more comfortable cottages in the eastern counties you may often see laid out before the fire a mat of peculiar construction which sometimes looks like a small mattress in difficulties. It is made from selvages and clippings, the refuse of the tailor's workshop; these strips of cloth are cut into lengths of two or three inches long by half an inch wide, and are knitted or tightly tied together with string, the variously coloured scraps being arranged in patterns according to the genius and taste of the artist. The complex structure when completed is stuffed with the clippings too small to be worked up on the outside, and the mass is then subjected to a process of thumping and stamping and pulling and hammering till at last there exudes—yes! that is the correct term, whatever you may say—a lumpy bundle, which in its pillowy and billowy entirety is called a hearthrug. The thing will last for generations, it never wears out, and it takes years of continuous stamping upon it before you can anyhow get it flat. It was one of these triumphs of industry that Mrs. Triplet desired to turn an honest penny by. Would her ladyship come and look at it *in situ*?

Now the lady shepherd is a woman of business, which the shepherd, notoriously, is not, and if she had gone alone no great harm would have come of the interview; but on that unlucky day the shepherd and his lady resolved to go together. That is a course which no shepherd and shepherdess should ever be persuaded to follow. Two men will often help one another when associated in a difficult enterprise; two women will almost always do better together than single-handed, but a man and a woman working together will always get in one another's way. On the occasion referred to the quick-witted old crone saw her chance in a moment, and commenced to play off one of her visitors against the other with consummate skill. From a hole beneath the narrow stairs she dragged the massive structure, and slowly unfolding it before our eyes commenced to stamp upon it in a kind of hideous demon dance, gazing at it fondly from time to time as if she could hardly bear to part with it.

In those days the fashion of wearing gay clothing had only just gone out among the male sex. For, less than forty years ago, we used to appear, on state occasions, in blue dress coats and brass buttons, and at great gatherings you might see green coats and brown ones, mulberry coats and chocolate ones, and there was a certain iridescence that gave a peculiarly sprightly look to an assembly even of males in those days, which has all passed away now. Hence when Mrs. Triplet displayed her *exhibit* we found ourselves gazing at a very gaudy spectacle. "There, lady! And I made the pattern all myself, I did. Many's the night I've laid awake thinking of it. Ah! them bottle-greens was hard to get, they was; gentlefolks has give up wearing greens. But that yaller rose, lady. Ain't *that* a yaller rose?" For once in her life the lady shepherd lost her nerve. Spasms of hysterical laughter wrestled within her, and her flushed face and contorted frame betrayed the conflict that was raging. How would it end? in the rupture of a vein or in shrieks of uncontrollable merriment? The shepherd was in terror; he stooped to the foolishest flattery; he went as near lying as a shepherd could without literally lying; but comedy changed to tragedy when from his lean purse he desperately plucked his very last sovereign, and giving it to that guileful old sorceress, ordered her to bring that hearth-rug to the parsonage without delay.

Next week—the very next week—came a pressing offer from another parishioner of another of these articles of home manufacture; next month came a third, though the price had dropped fifty per cent., which was accepted with exultant thankfulness. There was positively no stopping the activity of the new industry; until, before three months were over, six of these fearful contrivances had been all but forced upon us, one of them travelling to our door in a donkey-cart and one in a wheel-barrow—the lady shepherd being told she might have them at her own price, and pay for them at her own convenience—only have them she must: the makers could by no means take them away.

"Well, but you had nobody but yourselves to thank. How could you be so weak and silly?"

That may be very true. But do not our trials—our smaller trials—become so just because we have only ourselves to thank for them? We in the wilderness are exposed to temptations which go some way to make us silly and soft-hearted. Somehow, few of us are certain to keep our hearts as hard as the nether millstone. I do not pretend to be one of the seven sages: what I do say is that we country parsons have our trials.

It is, however, when the country parson has to buy a horse that he finds himself tried to the uttermost. Day after day, from all points of the compass, there appear at his gate the cunningest of the cunning and the sharpest of the sharp; and if at the end of a week the parson has not arrived at the settled conviction that he is three parts of a fool, it is impossible for him to dispute that the whole fraternity of horsey men feel no manner of doubt that he is so. Now, I don't like to be thought a fool: not many men do, unless they hope to gain something by it. The instinct of self-preservation or the hope of a kingdom might induce me to play the part of Brutus; but in my secret heart I should be buoyed up by the proud consciousness of superior wisdom. When, however, it comes to a long line of rogues—one after another for days and days without any collusion—continuing to tell you to your face, almost in so many words, that you certainly are a fool—it really ceases to be monotonous and becomes, after a while, vexatious. The fellows are so clever, too; they have such an enviable fluency of speech; they are possessed of such a rich fund of anecdote, such an easy play of fancy, such a readiness of apt illustration, and such a magnificent command of facial contortion, expressive of the subtlest movements of the heart and brain, that you cannot but feel how immeasurably inferior you are to the dullest of them in dialectic. But why should a man, when he asks you to try his charger, bring it round to the door-step, tempting you to get up on the off side?—what does he gain by it? Why should he tell you that "this hoss was a *twin* with that as Captain Dixie drives in his dog-cart"? Why should he assure you, upon his sacred honour, "that Roman nose will come square when the horse gets to be six years old—they always do"? or that "you always find bay horses turn chestnut if they're clipped badly"?

These men would not try these fictions upon any one else; why should I suffer for being a country parson by being told a long story—with the most religious seriousness—of "that there horse as Mr. Abel had, that stopped growing in his fore-quarters when he was two and went on growing with his hind-quarters till he was seven—that hoss that they called Kangaroo, 'cause he'd jump anything—anything under a church tower, only you had to give him his head"? I used to get much more irritated by this kind of thing when I was less mellowed by age than I am: and I have learnt to be more tolerant even of a horse-dealer than I once was. In an outburst of indignation one day, I turned angrily upon one of the fraternity, and said to him, "Man! how can you go on lying in this way; why won't you deal fairly, instead of always trying to take people in?" The man was not a bit offended—indeed he smiled quite kindly upon me. "Lor,' sir, do you suppose *we* never get took in?" I am fully persuaded that horse-dealer thought I was going to try the confidence trick with him.

*   *   *   *   *

I am often assured by my town friends that the *loneliness* of my country life must be very trying. I reply with perfect truth that I have never known what it is to feel lonely except in London. Some years ago one Sunday afternoon I was compelled to consult an eminent oculist. When the cab drove up to the great man's door in Cardross Square, his eminence was at the window in a brown study, with his elbows leaning on the wire blind, the tip of his nose flattened against the pane, his eyes vacantly staring at nothing. When we were shown into his presence, the forlorn and desolate expression on that forsaken man's face was quite shocking to the nerves. A painter who could have reproduced the look of aimless and despairing woe might have made a name for ever. When people talk to me of loneliness I always instinctively recall the image of that famous oculist in the heart of London on a Sunday afternoon. Ever since that day I have never been able to get over a horror of wire blinds. Happily, they are articles of furniture which have almost gone out now, but they used to be fearfully common. Even now the Londoner thinks it *de rigueur* to darken the windows of his sitting-room on the ground floor; and in furnished lodgings you must have wire blinds. Why is this? When I ask the question I am told that you *must* have wire blinds: if you didn't, people would look in. In the country we never have wire blinds, and yet nobody looks in; therefore you call our life lonely. But loneliness is not the simple product of external circumstances—it is the outcome of a morbid temperament, creating for itself a sense of vacuity, whatever may be a man's surroundings.

To sit on rocks, to muse on flood and fell,
To climb the trackless mountain, &c.

I suppose we all know that wishy-washy stuff, so there is no need to go on with the quotation.

What *is* trying in the country parson's life is its *isolation*. That is a very different thing from saying that he lives a lonely life. The parson who is conscientiously trying to do his duty in a country parish occupies a unique position. He is a man, and yet he must be something more than man, and something less too. He must be more than man in that he must be free from human passions and human weaknesses, or the whole neighbourhood is shocked by his frailty; he must be something less than man in his tastes and amusements and way of life, or there will be those who will be sure to denounce him as a worldling who ought never to have taken orders. If he be a man of birth and refinement, he is sure to be reported of as proud and haughty; if he be not quite a gentleman, he will be snubbed and flouted outrageously. The average country parson and his family has often to bear an amount of patronizing impertinence which is sometimes very trying. Even the squire and the parson do not always get on well together, and when they do not, the parson is very much at the other's mercy, and may be thwarted and worried and humiliated almost to any extent by a powerful, ill-conditioned, and unscrupulous landed proprietor. But it is from the come-and-go people who hire the country houses which their owners are compelled to let, that we suffer most. Not that this is always the case, for it not unfrequently happens that the change in the occupancy of a country mansion is a clear gain socially, morally, and intellectually to a whole neighbourhood—when, in the place of a necessitous Squire Western, and his cubs of sons and his half-educated daughters, drearily impecunious, but not the less self-asserting and supercilious, we get a family of gentle manners and culture and accomplishments, and lo! it is as sunshine after rain. But sometimes the new comers are a grievous infliction. Town-bred folk who emerge from the back streets and have amassed money by a new hair-wash or an improvement in sticking-plaster. Such as these are out of harmony with their temporary surroundings: they giggle in the faces of the farmers' daughters, ridicule the speech and manners of the labourers and their wives, and grumble at everything. They cannot think of walking in the dirty lanes, they are afraid of cows, and call children nasty little things. These people's hospitalities are very trying.

"Come, my boy. Have a cut at the venison. Don't be afraid. You shall have a good dinner for once; sha'n't he, my dear? and as much champagne as you like to put inside you?" It was a bottle-nosed Sir Gorgious Midas who spoke, and his lady at the other end of the table gave me a kindly wink as she caught my eye. But the wine was Gilby's, and not his best. These are the people who demoralize our country villages. They introduce a vulgarity of tone quite indescribable, and the rapidity of the change wrought in the sentiments and language of the rustics is sometimes quite wonderful.

The rustics don't like these come-and-go folk, but they get dazzled by them notwithstanding; they resent the airs which the footmen and ladies' maids give themselves, but nevertheless they envy them and think, "There's my gal Polly—she'd be a lady if she was to get into sich a house as that!" When they hear that up at the hall they play tennis on Sunday afternoons, the old people are perplexed, and wonder what the world is coming to; the boys and girls begin to think that *their* jolly time is near, when they too shall submit to no restraint, and join the revel rout of scoffers. The sour puritan snarls out, "Ah! there's your gentlefolks, they don't want no religion, they don't—and we don't want no gentlefolks!" For your sour puritan somehow has always a lurking sympathy with the Socialist programme, and it's honey and nuts to him to find out some new occasion for venting his spleen at the things that are. But one and all look askance at the parson, and inwardly chuckle that he is not having a pleasant time of it. "Our Reverend's been took down a bit, since that young gent at the Hall lit his pipe in the church porch. 'That ain't seemly,' says parson. 'Dunno about that,' says the tother, 'but it *seems* nice.'" Chorus, half-giggle, half-sniggle.

Do not the scientists teach that no two atoms are in absolute contact with each other; that some interval separates every molecule from its next of kin? Certainly this is inherent in the office and function of the country parson, that he is not *quite* in touch with any one in his parish if he be a really earnest and conscientious parson. He is too good for the average happy-go-lucky fellow who wants to be let alone. There is nothing to gain by insulting him. "He's that pig-headed he don't seem to mind nothing—only swearing at him!" You cannot get him to take a side in a quarrel. He speaks out very unpleasant truths in public and private. He occupies a social position that is sometimes anomalous. He has a provoking knack of taking things by the right handle. He does not believe in the almighty dollar, as men of sense ought to believe; and he is usually in the right when it comes to a dispute in a vestry meeting because he is the only man in the parish that thinks of preparing himself for the discussion beforehand. This isolation extends not merely to matters social and intellectual; it is much more observable in the domain of sentiment. A rustic cannot at all understand what *motive* a man can possibly have for being a bookworm; he suspects a student of being engaged in some impious researches. "To hear that there Reverend of ours in the pulpit you might think we was all right. But, bless you! he ain't same as other folk. He do keep a horoscope top o' his house to look at the stares and sich."

Not one man in a hundred of the labourers reads a book, and only when a book is new with a gaudy outside does he seem to value it even as a chattel. That any one should ever have any conceivable use for a big book is to him incomprehensible.

"If I might be so bold, sir," said Jabez, an intelligent father of a family with some very bright children who are "won'erful for'ard in their larning," "If I might be so bold, might I ask if you've really *read* all these grit books?" "No, Jabez; and I should be a bigger dunce than I am if I ever tried to. I keep them to *use*; they're my tools, like your spade and hoe. What's that thing called that I saw in your hand the other day when you were working at the draining job? You don't often use that tool I think, do you?" "Well, no. But then we don't get a job o' draining now same as we used. I mean to say as a man may go ten years at a stretch and never lay a drain-tile." "Well, then how about the use of his tools all this time?" Jabez smiled, slowly put his hand to his head, saw the point, and yet didn't see it. "But, lawk sir! that's somehow different. I can't see what yow *can du* wi' a grit book like this here." It was a massive volume of Littré's great dictionary, which I had just taken down to consult; it certainly did look portentous. "Why, Jabez, that's a dictionary—a French dictionary. If I want to know all about a French word, you know, I look it up here. Sometimes I don't find exactly what I want; then I go to *that* book, which is another French dictionary; and if...." I saw by the blank look in honest Jabez' face that it was all in vain. "Want to know ... all about ... words.... Why you ain't agoing to fix no drain-tiles with them sort o' things. Now that du wholly pet me aywt, that du."

I think no one who has not tried painfully to lift and lead others can have the least notion of the difficulty which the country parson has to contend with in the extreme thinness of the stratum in which the rural intellect moves. Since the schools have given more attention to geography, and since emigration has brought us now and then some entertaining letters from those who have emigrated to "furren parts," the people have slowly learnt to think of a wider area of *space* than heretofore they could imagine. Though even now their notions of geography are almost as vague as their notions of astronomy; I have never seen a map in an agricultural labourer's cottage. But their absolute ignorance of history amounts to an incapacity of conceiving the reality of anything that may have happened in past time. What their grandfathers have told them, that is to them history—everything before that is not so much as fable; it is not romance, it is a formless void, it is chaos. The worst of it is that they have no curiosity about the past. The same is true of their knowledge of anything approaching to the rudiments of physical science; it simply does not exist. A belief in the Ptolemaic system is universal in Arcady. I suspect that they think less about these things than they did. "That there old Gladstone, lawk! he's a deep un he is! He's as deep as the Pole Star he is!" said Solomon Bunch to me one day. "Pole Star?" I asked in surprise, "Where is the Pole Star, Sol?" "Lawks! I dunno; I've heard tell o' the Pole Star as the deep un ever sin' I was a booy!'

It is this narrowness in their range of ideas that makes it so hard for the townsman to become an effective speaker to the labourers. You could not make a greater mistake than by assuming you have only to use plain *language* to our rustics. So far from it, they love nothing better than sonorous words, the longer the better. It is when he attempts to make his audience follow a chain of reasoning that the orator fails most hopelessly, or when he comes to his illustrations. The poor people *know* so little, they read nothing, their experience is so confined, that one is very hard put to it to find a simile that is intelligible.

"Young David stood before the monarch's throne. With harp in hand he touched the chords, like some later Scald he sang his saga to King Saul!" It really was rather fine—plain and simple too, monosyllabic, terse, and with a musical sibillation. Unfortunately one of the worthy preacher's hearers told me afterwards with some displeasure that "he didn't hold wi' David being all sing-songing and scolding, he'd no opinion o' that." The stories of the queer mistakes which our hearers make in interpreting our sermons are simply endless, sometimes almost incredible. Nevertheless, no invention of the most inveterate story-teller could equal the facts which are matters of weekly experience.

"As yow was a saying in your sarment, 'tarnal mowing won't du wirout 'tarnal making—yow mind that! yer ses, an' I did mind it tu, an' we got up that hay surprising!" Mr. Perry had just a little misconceived my words. I had quoted from Philip Van Arteveldt. "He that lacks time to mourn, lacks time to mend. Eternity mourns that."

Not many months ago I was visiting a good simple old man who was death-stricken, and had been long lingering on the verge of the dark river. "I've been a thinking, sir, of that little hymn as you said about the old devil when he was took bad. I should like to hear that again." I was equal to the occasion.

The devil was sick—the devil a saint would be;The devil got well—not a bit of a saint was he!

[It was necessary to soften down the language of the original!]

"Is that what you mean?" Yes! it was that. "Well I've been a thinking, if the old devil had laid a bit longer and been afflicted same as some on 'em, as he'd a been the better for it. Ain't there no more o' that there little hymn, sir?"

The religious talk of our Arcadians is sometimes very trying—trying I mean to any man with only too keen a sense of the ludicrous, and who would not for the world betray himself if he could help it.

It is always better to let people welcome you as a friend and neighbour, rather than as a clergyman, even at the risk of being considered by the "unco guid" as an irreverent heathen. But you are often pulled up short by a reminder more or less reproachful, that if you have forgotten your vocation your host has not; as thus:—

"Ever been to Tombland fair, Mrs. Cawl?" Mrs. Cawl has a perennial flow of words, which come from her lips in a steady, unceasing, and deliberate monotone, a slow trickle of verbiage with never the semblance of a stop.

"Never been to no fairs sin' I was a girl bless the Lord nor mean to 'xcept once when my Betsy went to place and father told me to take her to a show and there was a giant and a dwarf dressed in a green petticoat like a monkey on an organ an' I ses to Betsy my dear theys the works of the Lord but they hadn't ought to be shewed but as the works of the Lord to be had in remembrance and don't you think sir as when they shows the works of the Lord they'd ought to begin with a little prayer?"

*   *   *   *   *

There is one salient defect in the East Anglian character which presents an almost insuperable obstacle to the country parson who is anxious to raise the *tone* of his people, and to awaken a response when he appeals to their consciences and affections. The East Anglian is, of all the inhabitants of these islands, most wanting in native courtesy, in delicacy of feeling, and in anything remotely resembling romantic sentiment. The result is that it is extremely difficult, almost impossible, to deal with a genuine Norfolk man when he is out of temper. How much of this coarseness of mental fibre is to be credited to their Danish ancestry I know not, but whenever I have noticed a gleam of enthusiasm, I think I have invariably found it among those who had French Huguenot blood in their veins. Always shrewd, the Norfolk peasant is never tender; a wrong, real or imagined, rankles within him through a lifetime. He stubbornly refuses to believe that hatred in his case is blameworthy. Refinement of feeling he is quite incapable of, and without in the least wishing to be rude, gross, or profane, he is often all three at once quite innocently during five minutes' talk. I have had things said to me by really good and well-meaning men and women in Arcady that would make susceptible people swoon. It would have been quite idle to remonstrate. You might as well preach of duty to an antelope. If you want to make any impression or exercise any influence for good upon your neighbours, you must take them as you find them, and not expect too much of them. You must work in faith, and you must work upon the material that presents itself. "The sower soweth the word." The mistake we commit so often is in assuming that because we sow—which is our duty—therefore we have a right to reap the crop and garner it. "It grows to guerdon after-days."

Meanwhile we have such home truths as the following thrown at us in the most innocent manner.

"Tree score? Is that all you be? Why there's some folk as 'ud take you for a hundred wi' that *hair* o' yourn!"

Mr. Snape spoke with an amount of irritation which would have made an outsider believe I was his deadliest foe; yet we are really very good friends, and the old man scolds me roundly if I am long without going to look at him. But he has quite a fierce repugnance to grey hair. "You must take me as I am, Snape," I replied; "I began to get grey at thirty. Would you have me dye my hair?" "Doy! Why that hev doyd, an' wuss than that—thet's right rotten thet is!"

Or we get taken into confidence now and then, and get an insight into our Arcadians' practical turn of mind. I was talking pleasantly to a good woman about her children. "Yes," she said, "they're all off my hands now, but I reckon I've had a expense-hive family. I don't mean to say as it might not have been worse if they'd all lived, and we'd had to bring 'em all up, but my meaning is as they never seemed to die convenient. I had twins once, and they both died, you see, and we had the club money for both of 'em, but then one lived a fortnight after the other, and so that took two funerals, and that come expense-hive!"

It is very shocking to a sensitive person to hear the way in which the old people speak of their dead wives or husbands exactly as if they'd been horses or dogs. They are *always* proud of having been married more than once. "You didn't think, Miss, as I'd had five wives, now did you? Ah! but I have though—leastways I buried five on 'em in the churchyard, that I did—and *tree on 'em beewties*!"3 On another occasion I playfully suggested, "Don't you mix up your husbands now and then, Mrs. Page, when you talk about them?" "Well, to tell you the truth, sir, I really du! But my third husband, he *was* a man! I don't mix him up. He got killed, fighting—you've heerd tell o' that I make no doubt. The others warn't nothing to him. He'd ha' mixed them up quick enough if they'd interfered wi' him. Lawk ah! He'd 'a made nothing of 'em!"

Instances of this obtuseness to anything in the nature of poetic sentiment among our rustics might be multiplied indefinitely. Norfolk has never produced a single poet or romancer.4 We have no local songs or ballads, no traditions of valour or nobleness, no legends of heroism or chivalry. In their place we have a frightfully long list of ferocious murderers: Thurtell, and Tawell, and Manning, and Greenacre, and Rush, and a dozen more whose names stand out pre-eminent in the horrible annals of crime. The temperament of the sons of Arcady is strangely callous to all the softer and gentler emotions.

*   *   *   *   *

There still remains something to say. In the minor difficulties with which the country parson has to deal, there is usually much that is grotesque, and this for the most part forces itself into prominence. When this is so, a wise man will not dwell too much upon the sad and depressing view of the situation; he will try and make the best of things as they are. There are trials that are, after all, bearable with a light heart. Unhappily there are others that make a man's heart very heavy indeed, partly because he thinks they need not be, partly because he can see no hope of remedy. It is of these I hope to speak hereafter.

II.
THE TRIALS OF A COUNTRY PARSON.

"Ther's times the world does look so queer,
Odd fancies come afore I call 'em,
An' then agin, for half a year,
No preacher 'thout a call's more solemn."

IN speaking of the trials of the country parson's life in my last essay, I left much unsaid that needed saying. I rather shrank from dealing with matters which are outside the range of my own experience, and confined myself to such illustrations of the positions maintained as my own personal knowledge could supply. There are, however, some phases of the country parson's life which I am perhaps less competent to dwell on than others who have been all their lives *rustics*, and because I would not willingly wound the feelings of those whom I honour and respect, therefore I am inclined to hang back and hold my peace and say nothing.

Why does not somebody else step in and take up the thread where I dropped it, deliver his testimony, and give us the record of his larger experience? Or shall we ask another question? How is it that people who have much to tell, so often have no faculty of setting it down in words and sentences? We boast of our advance in education, and yet what has it done for us—what is it doing for us?

I mean my son to be *really* educated. I mean him to be able to sit down to an organ and satisfy his soul as he dreams his dreams or sends forth his wail of aspiration, or sobs out his grief and penitence, or laughs forth his ecstasy of rapture, now in a passion of melody, now in subtle tangle of mysterious fugue, now in awful billows of harmony, making full concert to the angelic symphony. I mean him to be able to catch the laugh of the child, or the scowl of the ruffian, or the smirk of the swindler, or the wonder and triumph and joy and pride of the maiden who has just listened to her lover's tale, or the sombre beauty of the aged when the twilight deepens and they are thinking of the dawn. I mean my son to have the power to catch these things, and to *hold* them and show them to me, saying, "Look! there they are for you and me to dwell on when we will." Then, and not till then, will that lad of promise have begun to be educated. But we—or such as I—what upstarts we are! We that talk badly, write worse, and fumble and bungle miserably with that beggarly vehicle of communication between man and man which we call language—that wretched *calculus* which serves just a very little way towards helping us to hold converse with men as foolish as ourselves, but leaves us helpless to make the throstle feel how much we love him, and which we fling aside as a mere burden when our hearts are dying in us with what we call our loneliness or our despair. Educated! Who is educated? Certainly not the man who, having his memory full of a vast assemblage of odds and ends, can no more bring them out and produce them in an intelligible shape than I can produce on canvas the face of yonder old beldame with the square jaw and the bushy brows and the blazing eyes, and that burlesque of a bonnet, square and round and oval at one and the same moment, and no more capable of being described in words than of being written out in musical notation.

Yet it is undeniable that the knack of Mr. Gigadibs is a convenient knack, and it is a pity that my friend Mr. Cadaverous has not got it; he is "of those who know." Gigadibs is of those who can juggle with the parts of speech, and very pretty jugglery it is. I envy Gigadibs whenever I am compelled to relate things at second hand; for who can help lying when he tries to bear evidence upon what others have seen and heard and felt—and worst of all—have reasoned about?

*   *   *   *   *

It may have been observed that when I began upon the subject of the country parson's trials, I dwelt first upon those annoyances and positive wrongs which he is compelled to submit to at the hands of the powers that be, and which may be classed under the head of Financial; and, secondly, upon such as are inherent in his position as a personage living a life apart from those among whom he has to discharge his peculiar duties.

As far as regards the mere peasant, this isolation is only what any one must expect who is brought into relations more or less intimate with a class socially and intellectually below or above his own. But there are villages and villages, and the differences between them are as great as between the East End of London and the West, between May Fair and Red Lion Square. The ideal village is a happy valley, where a simple people are living sweetly under the paternal care of a gracious landowner, benevolent, open-handed, large-hearted, devout, a man of wealth and culture, his wife a Lady Bountiful; his daughters the judicious dispensers of liberal charity; his house the home of all that is refining, cheering, elevating. There the happy parson always finds a cordial welcome, and all those social advantages which make life pleasant and serene for himself and his family. Parson and squire work together in perfect harmony, the rectory and the hall are but the greater and the lesser parts of a well-adjusted piece of machinery which moves on with no friction and never comes to a dead stop. This is the ideal village.

How different are the real villages, and how various! Take the case of my friend Burney's parish. An oblong surface through which a high road runs straight as a ruler—wide ditches dividing the fields, with never a hedge and never a tree—nine square miles of land with a population of 900 human beings, here and there collected into an ugly hamlet, each with a central alehouse, and a few feeble poplars looking as if they were ashamed of themselves. There is not a farmer in the parish who occupies 300 acres of land. There is not a squire's house within a radius of eleven miles from the rectory door. The nearest market town is six miles off, the nearest railway station five. Friend Burney has his house and garden and perhaps £350 a year to spend—that is quite the outside. Every morning he goes to his school a long mile off, every afternoon he has some one to "look after," to visit in sickness or sorrow, to watch or advise or comfort. One year with another he calculates that he has to walk at least 1,500 miles in the way of duty. As to the mere Sunday work, that needs no dwelling on; take it all in all, it is about the least *wearing* and least troublesome part of the parson's duties, always provided he puts his heart into it, and has some faculty for it. But in all that tract of country over which he is sometimes cruelly assumed to be no more than a spiritual overseer, among all those 900 people, there is not a single man, woman, or child that cares to talk to him, or ever does talk to him, about anything outside the parish and its concerns. Nay! I forgot the schoolmaster and his wife. They are young, intelligent, hopeful, and they came out of Yorkshire, and have something to say of their experience in the North. But they are just a little—undeniably a *little* sore, just a *little* touchy: they have a grievance. When they first came down to

X., Mrs. Rector did not leave her card on Mrs. Petticogges. It was a slight. It was hoity-toity, it was airified. That is not all; the farmers are not, as you may say, *cordial* with the schoolmaster; and Farmer Gay, the big man who holds 700 acres in the next parish and gives lawn-tennis parties, never had the grace to take any notice of the Petticogges, does not in fact *know* the Petticogges. Meanwhile, friend Burney is manager of the school, and by far the largest contributor to the funds, and day by day he is in and out, he and his daughters. But there is no time to talk or confer. The Petticogges have their hands full; when their day's work is over they have had enough of it. Round and round and round they go in the dreary mill; every now and then there is a new regulation of My Lords to worry them, a new book to get up, a new code to study. Then there are the pupil teachers to look after, and returns to make up, and all the dull routine which has to be got through.

How *can* an elementary schoolmaster in a remote country village be a reading-man, or what motive has he to get out of the narrow groove in which he has been brought up? The best teachers, as a rule, are they who know their work best and very little indeed outside it. "How is it that at Dumpfield they don't get a larger grant?" I asked one day of an inspector noted for his shrewdness and good sense. "Surely Coxe is by far the ablest and most brilliant teacher for miles round; he is almost a man of genius?" "Precisely so," was the reply, "the man's out of place. These brilliant men with a touch of genius are a nuisance in an elementary school. My dear fellow, never let a *man of views* come into your school. Keep him out. Beware of the being who is for revolutionizing spelling and grammar!"

Mr. Petticogge is not a man of genius, only a better sort of elementary schoolmaster, and entirely absorbed in his work. He, too, as all the members of his fraternity do, occupies a position of isolation, and between him and the parson there is just so much in common as to make each hold aloof from the other without making either of them congenial to their other neighbours. As for the rest of friend Burney's neighbours, take them in the gross, and you may say of them what the ticket-of-leave man said of the Ten Commandments; "They're rather a poor lot and you can't make much out of 'em." I know no class of men who are less sociable than the smaller farmers, as we reckon smallness in the East. I mean the men who hold a couple of hundred acres and under. It has often been laid to the charge of the great occupiers in West Norfolk and elsewhere that in the good times they were lavish beyond all reason in their hospitalities. I believe there never has been anything of the sort among the smaller men; they are not unfriendly, they are not wanting in cordiality, but they are not companionable.

It is my privilege to know some who are notable exceptions to the all but universal rule. I have not far to go from my own door to find one whom I never pay a visit to without pleasure and profit, one who has for many years been a great reader of Lord Tennyson's poems, has strong opinions on politics and the questions of the day, a thoughtful, resolute, and true-hearted woman, who farms a hundred acres of land without a bailiff, and, among other evidences of her good taste and intelligence, is a diligent reader of the *Spectator*. But such are few and far between.

It is one of the trials of the country parson that, as soon as he passes out of the stratum to which the labourer belongs, he finds himself in a stratum where there is nothing that has any of the interest of originality, picturesqueness, or even passion. The people who live and move in that stratum are dismally like the ticket-of-leave man's ten commandments. My neighbours hardly believe me when I tell them I can see, even among the smaller farmers, much to admire, much to respect, and something to love; but I do not wonder that many a country parson "can't make much out of 'em." These men are having rather a hard life just now, but they have *not* to learn the most elementary lessons of thrift and frugality. As a class they have always practised these virtues, and as a class they are far less complaining than those who belong to the higher stratum; they bear their burdens silently, perhaps too silently, and they tell you that it's no good grumbling—"that," one of them said to me, "only makes things worse, 'cause it makes *you* worse!" Take them all in all, they whom I have elsewhere called *the little ones* are usually those of his parishioners with whom the parson seldom comes into unpleasant relations; they are usually very hard at work, very practical, very straightforward, and very seldom indeed prone to give themselves airs.

It is often very different with the large occupiers. In the good times the large farmers must have made very large profits, the percentage upon the actual capital embarked (unless my information has been strangely untrue, and the calculations that have been laid before me strangely inaccurate) being in many cases larger even than that which the shipowners earned in *their* good times. Is it to be wondered at that they became frequently intoxicated by their success, and got to believe that they were a superior order on whom the welfare of the nation depended? Or, again, can we be surprised that their awakening from their dream has not been pleasurable, and has somewhat soured them? Ten years ago a *gentleman farmer*—and every man who farmed 500 acres was a gentleman farmer—looked down upon the retail tradesman as quite beneath him in station, and regarded the parson as a respectable official whom it was the right thing to support, though he might care very little for him and his ways. In those days the farmer's sons and the parson's were frequently schoolfellows; the young people drew together, and the farmer's pupils too were another link between the farmhouse and the rectory. The bad seasons and the fall in prices came together, and the collapse was very rapid. But in nine cases out of ten, whereas the farmer's losses meant a disastrous abatement which extended over his *whole* income, the parson felt the pinch only in the fall of the tithe or in the rent of his glebe. His private fortune, being for the most part settled, remained as it was before. In East Anglia not 5 per cent. of the clergy are living upon the income of their benefices; but I should be very much surprised to find that 5 per cent. of the tenant-farmers have any considerable investments outside their working capital. The result is, that though the clergy have suffered quite severely enough, they have not suffered nearly so much as the farmers. The one has had to submit to a painful loss of professional income, and has had to fall back upon his private resources; the other has too often found himself with his credit balance approaching the vanishing point, the trade profit has been *nil*, and there have been no dividends from investments outside the going concern to keep up the old style or meet the old expenditure. When neighbours have been in the habit of meeting on equal terms, and one goes on pretty much as before, while the other has become a trifle shabby, and has to consider every shilling that he spends, it is almost inevitable that the poorer of the two should feel less cordial than before. He revenges himself upon the laws of the universe by proclaiming that there is wrong and injustice somewhere. Why is he on the brink of ruin while the parson has only knocked off his riding horse, or ceased to take his annual trip to the Continent, or lessened his establishment by a servant, or it may be two? He forgets that his neighbour is living upon the interest of realized property, and that he himself has to live upon what he can make, and upon that alone.

But what irritates the farmer most is that, at the worst, the parson is getting *something* out of the land while he is getting little or nothing; and though he knows as well as any one else that the tithe stands for a first mortgage upon the land, or for an annuity charged upon the land, which takes precedence of every other payment; and though he knows also that, in too many instances, he has himself to pay interest on the capital with which he has been pursuing his business, and that this interest has to be provided for whether that business is carried on at a profit or a loss, yet he persists in trying to convince himself that he was "let in" when he made himself liable for the tithes; he tells you he has "to pay the parson," and he does not like it. The parson is always *en évidence*, the landlord is out of the way—almost an abstraction, as the Government is; the agent *must* be submitted to, so must the tax gatherer. But the parson, could he not be got rid of? Granted that it would all come to the same in the end, and that if you could eliminate the parson the tithe would be laid on to the rent sooner or later, yet it might be very much later, and the end might be a long way off, and in the meantime he, the farmer, would put the tithe into his own pocket and into that of no one else. Hence there smoulder in the minds of many the smoky embers of discontent, and there is a coldness between the former friends. We are conscious of it, but we see no cure at present. When the tithe comes to be paid by the landlord, there may be a return to the old friendliness; but the *gratia male sarta* always leaves traces of the rift. I forbear from dwelling any longer upon this branch of the subject. When men are sore and in danger of becoming soured, then is the time for exercising a wise and tender reserve.

So far I have dealt with those trials which the country parson is exposed to from without; that is, such as arise from his intercourse with the wicked world—the wicked world that puts its cruel claw into his pocket, or growls at him, or glares at him, or frightens him, or laughs at him, or tries to gobble him up. But his trials do not end there. He has relations with another world—that professional world to which he belongs in another sense than that by which he is regarded as a citizen. As a clergyman he is a member of a class, a profession, a clique if you will, which has a coherence and a homogeneity such as no other profession can lay claim to, not even the profession of the law. The lawyer may be half a dozen things at the same time—a trader, a politician, a practical agriculturist, a land agent, a coroner, a steeple-chase rider, a general Jack-pudding. Everything brings grist to his mill, and the more irons he has in the fire the larger will be the number and the more varied the character of his clients. But the parson must be a clergyman, and a clergyman only; he is, so to speak, confined within the four walls of his clerical associations, and if he steps beyond them he is always regarded with a certain measure of suspicion. Even literature, unless there be a distinctly theological flavour about it, he embarks in at his peril; a clergyman who writes books is looked askance at, as a person whose "heart isn't in his work." Of course we get "narrow-minded." We all go about with an iron mask weighing upon us—hiding our handsome features, interfering with our respiration, stunting our growth.

That is not all, though that is bad enough; we are all ticketed and labelled in a way that no other class is. Of late years it appears that the rising generation of clerics has begun to insist more and more upon the necessity of this professional exclusiveness, and desires to claim for itself the privileges of a *caste*. It shaves off its nascent whiskers and glories in a stubby cheek; it dresses in a hideous garment, half petticoat, half frock, for the most part abominably ill made; above all, it rumples about its bullet head a slovenly abomination called a *wide-awake*, as if *that* would preserve it from all suspicion of being sleepy and stupid, and it adopts a tone and a vocabulary which shall be distinctive and as far as possible from the speech of ordinary Englishmen. "We must close up our ranks," said one of them to me, "close up our ranks and present a united front, and show the world that we are prepared to hang together, act together, march together. We have been atoms too long; we want coherence, my dear sir—coherence. We are moving towards the general adoption of the Catholic cassock!" "Do you mean to say," I answered, "that you will persist in sporting that emasculated felt turbanette till you arrive at the general adoption of the cassock? Then, in the name of all the lines of beauty, on with the cassock, but away with the wide-awake!" I'm afraid my young friend was hurt; suspected me of some covert profanity, and deplored my flagrant want of *esprit de corps*.

And yet I have been almost a worshipper of Burke from my boyhood, and was early so impregnated with the fundamental positions of the *Thoughts on the Causes of our present Discontents* that, if I only *could* choose my party, I should follow my leader to prison or to death, and do his bidding, ἀνδρείως καὶ μύσαντα, never looking behind me. Unhappily in matters political the curse of a flabby amorphous eclecticism is upon too many of us; watching the conflict of principles or policies in a dazed and bewildered frame of mind, we persuade ourselves that we are philosophically impartial when we are only indolently indifferent. "Which train are you going by, sir—up or down?" "I'll wait and see!" And both engines rush out and leave the unhappy vacillator to his reveries, till by-and-by the platform is cleared and the station is shut up for the night, and the gas lamps are turned down; and there is no moon and no stars and no shelter, and the wind is rising.

But ever since I have, so to speak, taken the shilling and entered the Church's service and put myself under orders, I have loyally stood up for my cloth, and I am quite willing to bear the reproaches of that service where there are any to bear. We clergy get a good deal of stupid and very vulgar ridicule hurled at us, and we cannot very well retaliate. It is a case of *Athanasius contra mundum*. The "world" is very big and rather unassailable, and we of the minority are apt to assume that we can afford to hold our peace, that we gain by turning the right cheek to him who smites us on the left, and that we should lose by giving a foul-mouthed liar and coward a drubbing and tossing him into the horse-pond. We stand upon the defensive. We have hardly any other choice. But it is rather trying to have to answer for all the sins, negligences, and ignorances, the follies and the bad taste of all who wear the wide-awake.

As far as the instances of downright wickedness and immorality go, I think nobody will pretend that any class in the community can show such a clean bill of health as the clergy. As I look round me upon my clerical brethren of all ages and all opinions, I can honestly say I do not know one of them whose daily life is not free from reproach or suspicion. During all my life I have never myself known more than one beneficed clergyman who was a real black sheep. That there are such men of course I cannot doubt, but their aggregate number constitutes, I am sure, a very small percentage of the class which they disgrace by being included in it. Surely it is very trying and very irritating to have such instances brought up against you, not as rare exceptions, but as examples of the general rule.

Our Nonconformist neighbours know all about such cases, and cannot understand why they should exist. They know that a Wesleyan or a Congregational minister who should underlie any grave suspicion would infallibly disappear from the neighbourhood in a week. Why should the rector of Z——, whose intemperance has been clearly proved, be allowed to return to his parish after his term of suspension, and begin again to minister among the same people whose sense of decency he has outraged till it was past all bearing? You tell your Nonconformist friend that it cannot be helped because the reverend sot has got a freehold in his benefice. "Oh, it can't be helped, can't it?" he answers; "that's it, is it? The law ain't to blame, and the bishop ain't to blame, and the churchwardens ain't to blame, and, according to that, the parson ain't to blame neither, except that the old fool's been and got found out." These people know that such scandals are impossible at the chapels; they are not impossible at the churches; they know that the deacons, and the elders, and the conference, or whatever the power may be that keeps up the discipline, comes down with swift severity in the one case, and the rural dean and archdeacons and the bishops are all but powerless in the other. In many cases the influence of a bad example, or the memory of a shameful reputation, is avoided by giving an incumbent indefinite leave of absence; but this is, after all, only a confession of weakness, and the fact that the parson still takes the income of the benefice, though his work is done by another, that itself is a scandal. Ecclesiastical reformers, lay or clerical, who stop short of dealing with the subject of the parson's freehold, are merely hacking and lopping the branches in the vain hope of saving the tree. If the thing is rotten, let it die placidly, or let it be cut down bravely. Where you have not the pluck to do the one thing, why fidget about the other?

Happily, however, we are not much troubled with "criminous clerks," we country parsons. The regular out-and-out bad ones usually retire into holes and corners, and they are but few and far between. We hear of them much more from our Meetingers than from any one else. The Meetinger keeps himself posted up with the last clerical escapade, and fires it off at us when he gets a chance, and the old argument has to be gone over again, and the parson goes home feeling that he was born to be badgered, and that he must expect it even to the end of the world.

It may seem strange to the inexperienced, but it is none the less true, that we suffer a great deal more from the best of our brethren than we do from the worst. They are the over-zealous, who are determined to change the face of the world and revolutionize society and reform everything, and improve everybody, and who cannot leave things alone to develop and grow, who make their fellow-creatures' lives a burden to them. When we are young we have such unbounded faith in ourselves, and such unbounded ignorance and inexperience. The world is all before us, and all to conquer and remodel; our seniors are sad fogeys, so slow, so stiff, so cautious. There is so much dust everywhere and upon everything. Our brooms are so new, so swishy, and our arms so strong. We have our wits about us, and our senses all keen and sharp. We find it hard to believe that we have not been called into being to do a great deal of sweeping and getting rid of cobwebs. I love to see the young fellows all bubbling over with energy, and all aflame with fiery zeal; I would not have it otherwise. God bless them! say I, but they do rout us about very uncomfortably, and they are very foolish.

It was only the other day that I was asked to go and visit a church to which a very hurricane of a man had been recently appointed, and which he had already set himself to restore. He knew no more about church architecture than I do about Sanskrit, and less about history than I do about chemistry. He had a small army of bricklayers picking and slopping about the sacred edifice, tearing down this and digging up that and smalming over the other. And this reverend worthy had not even consulted the parish clerk! "Of course you have had a faculty for all this?" I suggested.

"Not I! Faculty indeed! I have to save all the expense I can. I have made up my mind to have nothing whatever to do with any officials or professionals of any sort or kind; I'm my own architect!"

Now, if a man chooses to be his own tailor, nobody will be much the worse and nobody will much care; but when a man sets himself to "restore" a church by the light of nature, it is a much more serious matter, and it is almost beyond belief what a brisk and bouncing young fellow, with the best intentions, and an immeasurable fund of ignorance to fall back upon, can do without any one interfering with him. You tell him he'll get into a scrape—that the bishop will be down upon him—that there are such things as law courts. He smiles the benevolent smile of superior wisdom, and dashes on with heroic valour. If he calls himself a Ritualist, he gets rid of the Jacobean pulpit, or the royal arms, or the ten commandments, and sets up a construction which he calls a reredos, all tinsel and putty and *papier mâché*; hurls away the old pews before you know where you are, nails the brasses to the walls, sets up a lectern, and intones the service, keeping well within the chancel, from which he firmly banishes all worshippers who are not males. As for that gallery at the west end where the singers used to sit for a couple of centuries, and never failed to take their part with conscious pride in their own performances, that is abomination in his eyes—that must go of course, "to throw out the belfry arch, you see, and to bring the ringers into closer connection with the worship of the sanctuary." "I love to see the bell ropes," said one of these dear well-meaning young clergymen to me. "They are a constant lesson and reminder to us, my friend. Did you ever read Durandus on Symbolism? That is a very precious observation of his, that a bell rope symbolises humility—it always hangs down."

But if an energetic young reformer calls himself an Evangelical, he is, if possible, a more dangerous innovator than the other. Then the axes and hammers come in with a vengeance. None of your pagan inscriptions for him, teaching false doctrine and popery. None of your *Orate pro anima*, none of your crosses and remains of frescoes on his walls; St. Christopher with the Child upon his shoulder wading through the stream, St. Sebastian stuck all over with arrows, or St. Peter with those very objectionable keys. As for the rood screen, away with it! Are we not all kings and priests? If you must have a division between the chancel and the nave, set up the pulpit there, tall, prominent, significant; and if the preacher can't be heard, then learn the lesson which our grandfathers taught us, and let there be a sounding-board.

The serious part of all this passionate meddling with the *status quo ante* is that any young incumbent can come in and play the wildest havoc with our old churches without any one interfering with him. The beneficed cleric is master of the situation, and is frightfully more so now that Church rates have been abolished than he was before. It is no one's interest to open his mouth; is he not *inducted* into possession of the sacred building, and is he not therefore tenant for life of the freehold? As long as he makes himself liable for all the expense, it is surely better to let him have his way. "I ain't a going to interfere," says one after another; and in six weeks a church which had upon its walls and floors, upon its tower and its roof, upon its windows and its doors, upon its every stone and timber, the marks and evidences which constituted a continuous chronicle, picturing—not telling—a tale of the faith and hope, and folly and errors, and devotion and sorrow, and striving after a higher ideal and painful groping for more light in the gloom—a tale that goes back a thousand years, a tale of the rude forefathers of the village world which still regards the house of God as somehow its own—in six weeks, I say, all this is as effectually obliterated as if a ton of dynamite had been exploded in one of the vaults, and the genius of smugness had claimed the comminuted fragments as her own.

Then there is the mania for decorations too. I like to see them; I am sure the new fashion has been the occasion for awakening a great deal of interest in, and something approaching proud affection for, our old churches; but here again people, with every desire to be reverential and to do the right thing, succeed amazingly in doing just the wrong one. Have I not seen a most beautiful fourteenth-century rood screen literally riddled with tin tacks and covered with various coloured paper roses, festooned in fluffy frills of some cheap material on which languid dandelions and succulent bluebells lolled damply at the Eastertide? Next time I saw that exquisite work of art, lo! there was a St. Lawrence with his eye put out and two holes in his forehead, and between the lips of a St. Barbara, who for her loveliness might have been painted by Carlo Crivelli, there protruded a bent nail which looked for all the world like an old tobacco pipe. Who can "restore" that precious rood screen or repair the damage wrought in an hour by the *decorators* turned loose into that meek little church a year ago?

I think the average laymen who live in the towns can have very little notion of what the parson suffers when he finds himself turned into a church in which he has to officiate for the rest of his life, and which his predecessor has mauled and mangled and murdered, leaving no more life in it than there is among the wax figures at Madame Tussaud's.

"But do not these rash and furious young zealots of whom you have spoken burn their fingers sometimes, and does not the bishop sometimes come down upon them?" Yes! very often, *after the mischief has been done*. I knew one monster who upon his glebe had some seven of the noblest oak trees in the county of Norfolk. *Lucus ligna* was his view of the case, and he sold them all. Down they came every tree of them. Some said he wanted to see how the landscape would look without them, some that he wanted to go to Norway, and there are plenty of trees there. The patron of the living called that man to account, and I am told made him disgorge the proceeds of his ill-gotten gains; and the bishop is generally believed to have sent him a mandate to put back those trees in their former position. But that clerical monster, though he plays the fiddle to put Amphion to shame, has never learnt Amphion's tune or cared to charm back the giant vegetables that were once the pride and glory of the countryside. In the days when the wicked received their reward in this world a thousand evil-doers have been hanged for crimes incomparably less injurious to the community at large than that which lies to the charge of this reverend sinner; but he enjoys the income of his benefice to this day, and grows willows instead of oaks, not to turn to the use which Timon recommended to one of his visitors, but to turn into cash; for they grow fast, and the manufacturers of cricket bats are hard put to it to supply the demand for their wares.

What we want is to make it at least a misdemeanour punishable by imprisonment for the parson to touch the fabric of the church under any circumstances whatever, except with the consent and under the license of some external authority. But that implies that the ownership of the church should no longer be vested in a *corporation sole*. It brings us again face to face with the whole question of the parson's freehold, and how long is that mischievous legal fiction—which is, however, a very stubborn legal fact—to be endured?

If I were to go on in this vein, and dwell upon all the parson has to suffer from his *predecessors*—the man who built the house two miles from the parish church; the man who added to it to find room for a score of pupils; the man who loved air, or the man who loved water, or the man who loved society, or the man who bred horses, or the man who turned the rectory into a very lucrative lunatic asylum—I should tire out my reader's patience, and the more so that there are other trials about which it is advisable that I should utter my querulous wail.

I know one clergyman who, though ordained some forty years ago, has never written or preached a sermon in his life; but I only know one. His is perhaps a unique case. As a rule, we all begin by being curates—that is, we begin by learning our business as subordinates. It would be truer to say we used to begin that way; but subordination is dying out all over the world, and in the ministry of the Church of England subordination is a virtue which is *in articulo mortis*. Nowadays a young fellow at twenty-three, who has become a reverend gentleman for just a week, poses at once as the guide, philosopher, and friend of the whole human race. He poses as a great teacher. It is not only that he delivers the oracles with authoritative sententiousness from the tripod, but he has no doubts and no hesitation about anything in earth or heaven. He fortifies himself with a small collection of brand-new words which you, poor ignorant creature, don't know the meaning of. You feel rather "out of it" when he gravely calls your gloves *Mannaries* (he does not wear them), and your dressing-gown a *Poderis*; expresses his mournful regret that there is no *Scuophylacium* in the *Presbytery*, nor any *Bankers* on the walls; gently admonishes you for standing bareheaded by the grave at your time of life, when prudence would suggest, and ecclesiastical precedent would recommend, the use of the *Anabata*; tells you he always goes about with a *Totum* under his arm, and a *Virge* in his right hand. When he vanishes you slyly peep into your Du Cange, but the *Bankers* are quite too much for you.

I am not much more ignorant than other men of my age, but I never did pretend to omniscience, and when I don't know a thing I am not ashamed of asking questions. But our modern curates never ask questions. "Inquire within upon everything," seems to be stamped upon every line of their placid faces. When I was a young curate I was very shy and timid, and held my dear rector in some awe. It might have been hoped that as the years went by I should have grown out of this weakness—

but no! I am horribly afraid of the *curates* now. I dare hardly open my mouth before my superiors, and that they are my superiors I should not for a moment presume to question. I know my place, and I tremble lest I should betray my silliness by speaking unadvisedly with my lips. All this is very trying to a man who will never see sixty again. The hoary head is no crown at all to the eyes of the young and learned. They don't yet cry out at me, "Go up, thou baldhead," but I can't help suspecting that they're only waiting to do it sooner or later. For myself I have, unfortunately, never been able to afford to engage the services of a clergyman who should assist me in my ministrations. So much the worse for me, and so much the worse for my parish. When I am no longer able to do my own pastoral work, I shall feel the pinch of poverty; but I am resolved to be very meek to my curate when he shall vouchsafe to take me under his protection. I will do as I am told.

It is a very serious fact, however, which we cannot but think of with anxiety, that since the *Curate Market* rose, as it did some fifteen or twenty years ago, there has been a large incursion of young men into the ministry of the Church of England who are not gentlemen by birth, education, sentiment, or manners, and who bring into the profession (regarded as a mere profession) no *capital* of any sort—no capital I mean of money, brains, culture, enthusiasm, or force of character. This is bad enough, but there is a worse behind it. These young curates almost invariably marry, and the last state of that man is worse than the first. My friends assure me, and my observation confirms it, that the domestic career of these young people is sometimes very pathetic. Sanguine, affectionate, simple-minded and childlike, they learn the hard lessons of life all too late, and their experience comes to them, as Coleridge said, "like the stern lights of a ship, throwing a glare only upon the path behind." When their children come upon them with the usual rapidity, it is but rarely that we country parsons keep these married curates among us. They emigrate into the towns for the sake of educating their progeny, or because they soon find out that there is no hope of preferment for them among the villages. When there is no family, or when the bride has brought her spouse some small accession of income, the couple stay where they are for years till somebody gives them a small living, and there they do as others do. But in the first exuberance of youth, and when the youthful pair are highly delighted with the position that has been acquired, *he* is profoundly impressed with the sense of his importance, and *she* exalted at the notion of having married a "clergyman and a gentleman;" *he* is apt to be stuck up, and *she* is very apt to be huffy. It's bad enough to be associated officially with an underbred man, but it's a great deal worse to find yourself brought into social relations, which cannot be avoided, with an underbred woman. The curate's wife is sometimes a very dreadful personage, but then most dreadful when she is a "young person" of your own parish who has angled for the clerical stickleback and landed him.

The Rev. Percy De la Pole was a courtly gentleman, sensitive, fastidious, and just a trifle, a little trifle, distant in his demeanour. His curate, the Rev. Giles Goggs, was a worthy young fellow enough, painstaking and assiduous, anxious to do his duty, and not at all airified. We all liked him till Rebecca Busk overcame him. Mr. De la Pole was cautious and reserved by temperament; but who has never committed a mistake? In an evil hour—how could he have been so imprudent?—he gently warned the curate against the wiles of Miss Busk and her family, telling him that she was far from being a desirable match, and going to the length of saying plainly that she was making very indelicate advances. "All that may be quite true," replied Mr. Goggs, "but I am sure you will soon change your opinion. I come in now to let you know that I am engaged to be married to Miss Busk." From that day our reverend neighbour had so bad a time of it that it is commonly believed his valuable life was shortened by his sufferings. I am afraid some people behaved very cruelly, for they could not help laughing. Mrs. Goggs took her revenge in the most vicious way. On all public occasions she clasped the rector's arm and looked up in his face with the tenderest interest. She tripped across lawns at garden parties to pluck him by the sleeve, screamed out with shrill delight when he appeared, called him her dear old father confessor, giggled and smirked and patted him, and fairly drove him out of the place at last by finding that he had twice preached borrowed sermons, and keeping the discovery back till the opportune moment arrived, when, at a large wedding party, she shook her greasy little ringlets at him with a wicked laugh, exclaiming, "Ah! you dear old sly-boots, when you can speak like that why do you preach the Penny Pulpit to us?" The wretched victim could not hold up his head after that, and when a kind neighbour strongly advised him to dismiss the curate whose wife was unbearable, the broken-down old gentleman feebly objected. "My dear friend, I may have an opportunity of getting preferment for Mr. Goggs some day, but in the meantime I have no power to send away my curate because his wife—well, because his wife is *not nice*."

It often happens that the parson has to go away from his parish for some months, and he finds considerable difficulty in getting any one to take charge of it during his absence. At the eleventh hour he is compelled to take the last chance applicant. And behold, he and his parishioners are given over to a *locum tenens*. This is nothing more than saying that he has put himself into the power of a man with a loose end.

When the worthy rector of Corton-in-the-Brake had reached his fiftieth year, he obtained an accession of fortune and gave out that he intended to marry. He furnished his house anew at a great expense, and found no difficulty in getting a wife. Then he vowed that he would go to the south of France for the winter, and get a curate. He was a prim and punctilious personage, and he did not mean to deal shabbily with his substitute. But two things he insisted on: first, that this *locum tenens* should be married, and secondly that he should be childless. He got exactly the right man at last, a scholarly, well-dressed, and evidently accomplished gentleman, who spoke of Mrs. Connor with respectful confidence and affection, who had been married ten years, and had no family, who made no difficulties except that the stables were, he feared, inconveniently too small, but he would make shift. With a mind relieved and a blissful honeymoon before him, the Rev. John Morris set out for Nice—in the days when the railway system was not as complete as now—and the Rev. Mr. Connor arrived at the rectory the next Saturday afternoon. Mrs. Connor came too, with *fourteen brindled bulldogs*—young and old. That was her speciality, and she gave her whole mind to keeping the breed pure and making large sums by every litter. During the following week appeared seven pupils, the rejected of several public schools, who were committed to the care of Mr. Connor to be kept out of their parents' sight and to "prepare for the University." Mrs. Connor kept no female servants. Not a woman or a girl dared pass the rectory gate. The Connors had a man cook and *men housemaids*. The bulldogs would prowl about the neighbourhood in threes and fours with a slow shuffling trot, sniffing, growling, turning their hideous blood-shot eyes at you, undecided whether or not to tear you limb from limb; and then passing on with menacing contempt. Sometimes there were rumours of horrible fights; no one dared to separate the brutes except Mrs. Connor. Once the two mightiest of the bulldogs got "locked," as the head man expressed it. "What did you do?" "Do? Why I shrook out to Billy to hang on, and I called the Missus, and she gave 'em the hot un, and they give in!" The *hot un* turned out to be a thin bar of steel with a wooden handle which was always kept ready for use in the kitchen fire, and which Mrs. Connor had her own method of applying red hot so as to paralyze the canine culprit without blemishing him. But imagine the condition of that newly furnished parsonage when the poor rector came back to his home.

It is easy for everybody else to look only at the ludicrous side, but the clerical sufferer has to bear the real bitterness of such an experience, and to him the mere damage to his property is the least part of the business. Everybody says sulkily, "Why were we left to such a man as that?" For the country parson has to answer for all the sins and short-comings of those whom he leaves to represent himself; all their indiscretions, their untidiness, their careless reading, their bad preaching, their irreverence or their foolery, their timidity or their violence, their ignorance or their escapades. One man is horribly afraid of catching the measles; another "has never been accustomed to cows" and will not go where they are; a third is a woman-hater, and week by week bawls out strong language against the other sex, beginning with Eden and ending with Babylon. The absentee returns to find everything has been turned topsy-turvy. The *locum tenens* has set every one by the ears, altered the times of service, broken your pony's knees, had your dog poisoned for howling at the moon, or kept a monkey in your drawing-room. People outside laugh, but when you are the sufferer, and the conviction is forced upon you that harm has been done which you cannot hope to see repaired, you are not so likely to laugh as to do the other thing.

Shall I go on to dwell upon the aggrieved parishioner, the amenities of the School Board, the anxieties of the school treat, the scenes at the meetings of the Poor-law guardians, the faithful laity who come to expostulate, to ask your views and to set you right? Shall I? Shall I dwell upon the occasional sermons which some delegate from some society comes and fulminates against you and your people? Nay! Silence on some parts of our experience is golden.

*　　　*　　　*　　　*　　　*

When we have said all that need be said about the minor vexations and worries which are incident to the country parson's life, and which, like all men who live in isolation, he is apt to exaggerate, there is something still behind it all which only a few feel to be an evil at all, and which those who do feel, for many good reasons, are shy of speaking about; partly because they know it to be incurable, partly because if they do touch upon it they are likely to be tabulated among the dissatisfied, or are credited with unworthy motives which they know in their hearts that they are not swayed by.

That which really makes the country parson's position a cheerless and trying one is its absolute *finality*. Dante's famous line ought to be carved upon the lintel of every country parsonage in England. When the new rector on his induction takes the key of the church, locks himself in, and tolls the bell, it is his own passing bell that he is ringing. He is shutting himself out from any hope of a further career upon earth. He is a man transported for life, to whom there will come no reprieve. Whether he be the sprightly and sanguine young bachelor of twenty-four who takes the family living; or the podgy plebeian whose uncle the butcher has bought the advowson for a song; or the college tutor, fastidious, highly cultured, even profoundly learned, who has accepted university preferment; or the objectionable and quarrelsome man, whom it was necessary to provide for by "sending into the country";—be he who he may, gifted or very much the reverse, careless or earnest, slothful or zealous, genial, eloquent, wise, and notoriously successful in his ministrations, or the veriest stick and humdrum that ever snivelled through a homily— from the day that he accepts a country benefice he is a shelved man, and is put upon the retired list as surely as the commander in the navy who disappears on half-pay. I do not mean only that the country parson is never promoted to the higher dignities in the Church, or that cathedral preferment is very rarely bestowed upon him; but I do mean that he is never moved from the benefice in which he has once been planted. You may ply me with instances to the contrary here and there, but they are instances only numerous enough to illustrate the universality of the law which prevails—*Once a country parson always a country parson*; where he finds himself there he has to stay.

As long as the patronage of ecclesiastical preferment in the Church of England remains in the hands it has remained in for a thousand years and more, and as long as the tenure of the benefice continues to be as it is and as it has been since feudal times, I can see no remedy and no prospect that things should go on otherwise than they do now. Give a man some future in whatever position you put him, and he will be content to give you all his best energies, his time, his strength, his fortune, in return for the chance of recognition that he may sooner or later reasonably look forward to; but there is no surer way of making the ablest man a *fainéant* at the best, a soured and angry revolutionist at the second best, and something even more odious and degraded at the worst, than to shut him up in a cage like Sterne's starling, and bid him sing gaily and hop briskly from perch to perch till the end of his days, with a due supply of sopped bread crumbs and hemp seed found for him from hour to hour, and a sight of the outer world granted him—only through the bars.

There is a something which appeals to our pity in every *carrière manqué*. The statesman who made one false step, the soldier who at the crisis of his life was out-generalled, the lawyer who began so well but who proved not quite strong enough for the strain he had to bear—we meet them now and then where we should least have expected to find them, the obliterated heroes of the hour, and we say with a kindly sigh, "This man might have had another chance." But each of these has had his chance; they have *worked up* to a position and have forfeited it when it has been proved they were in the wrong place; they have gone into the battle of life, and the fortune of war has gone against them; tried by the judgment of that world which is so "cold to all that might have been," they have been found wanting; they have had to step aside, and make way for abler men than themselves. But up and down the land in remote country parsonages—counting by the hundreds—there are to be found those who have never had, and never will have, any chance at all of showing what stuff is in them—sometimes men of real genius shrivelled, men of noble intellect, its expansion arrested, men fitted to lead and rule, men of force of character and power of mind, who from the day that they entered upon the charge of a rural parish have had never a chance of deliverance from

The dull mechanic pacing to and fro, The set grey life and apathetic end.

You might as well expect from such as these that they should be able to break away from their surroundings, or fail to be dwarfed and cramped by them, as expect that Robinson Crusoe should develop into a sagacious politician.

"Pathos," did I say? How often have I heard the casual visitor to our wilds exclaim with half-incredulous wonder, "What, *that* Parkins? Why, he used to walk the streets of Camford like a god! He carried all before him. The younger dons used to say the world was at his feet—a ball that he might kick over what goal he might please to choose. And was that other really the great Dawkins, whose lectures we used to hear of with such envy, we of St. Chad's College, who had to content ourselves with little Smug's platitudes? Dawkins! How St. Mary's used to be crowded when he preached! Old Dr. Stokes used to say Dawkins had too much fire and enthusiasm for Oxbridge. He called him Savonarola, and he meant it for a sneer. And that's Dawkins! How are the mighty fallen!"

I lay innocent traps for my casuals now and then, when I can persuade some of the effaced ones to come and dine with us, but it is often just a little too sad. They are like the ghosts of the heroic dead. Men of sixty, old before their time; the broad massive brow, with the bar of Michael Angelo, is there, but— the eyes that used to flash and kindle have grown dim and sleepy, those lips that curled with such fierce scorn, or quivered with such glad playfulness or subtle drollery—it seems as if it were yesterday—have become stiff and starched. Poverty has come and hope has gone. Dawkins knew so little about the matter that he actually believed he only required to get a *pied à terre* such as a college living would afford him, and a (nominal) income of £700 a year, and there would be a fresh world to conquer as easy to subdue as the old Academic world which was under his feet. Poor Dawkins! Poor Parkins! Poor any one who finds himself high and dry some fine morning on his island home, while between him and the comrades who helped him to his fate the distance widens; for him there is no escape, no sailing back. There are the fruits of the earth, and the shade of the trees, and the wreckage of other barks that have stranded there; but there is no to-morrow with a different promise from to-day's, nor even another islet to look to when this one has been made the most of and explored, only the resource of acquiescence as he muses on the things that were,

Gazing far out foamward.

Such men as these I have in my mind were never meant to be straitened and poor. They never calculated upon six or eight children who have to be educated; the real dreariness of the prospect, its crushing unchangeableness only gradually reveals itself to them; they shut their eyes not so much because they will not as because they *cannot* believe that such as they have no future. Their first experience of life led up to the full conviction that character and brain-power *must* sooner or later bring a man to the first rank—what did it matter where a man cast anchor for a time? So they burnt their ships bravely, "hope like a fiery column before them, the dark side not yet turned." But suppose there was no scope for the brains and consequently no demand for them? We in the wilderness have abundance of butter and eggs, but *keep* these commodities long enough, and they infallibly grow a trifle stale.

People say with some indignation, "What a pity, what a shame, that Parkins and Dawkins should be buried as they are!" No, that is not the shame nor the pity; the shame is that, being buried, they should have no hope of being dug up again. Yonder splendid *larva* may potentially be a much more splendid *imago*; let it bury itself by all means, but do not keep it for ever below ground. Do not say to it, "Once there, you must stop there, there and there only. For such as you there shall be no change, your resting place shall inevitably be your grave."

But if it be a melancholy spectacle to see the wreck of a man of great intellect and noble nature, whom banishment in his prime and poverty in his old age have blighted; scarcely less saddening is the sight of the active and energetic young man of merely ordinary abilities to whom a country living has come in his youth and vigour, and once for all has stunted his growth and extinguished his ambition. There is no man more out of place, and who takes longer to fit into his place, than the worthy young clergyman who has been ordained to a town curacy, kept for four or five years at all the routine work of a large town parish, worked and admirably organized as—thank God!—most large town parishes are, and who, at eight or nine and twenty, is dropped down suddenly into a small village, and told that there he is to live and die. He does not know a horse from a cow. He has had his regular work mapped out for him by his superior officer as clearly as if he were a policeman. He has been part of a very complex machinery, religious, educational, eleemosynary. Every hour has been fully occupied, so occupied that he has lost all the habits of reading and study which he ever possessed. He has to preach at least one hundred sermons in the course of the year, and there is not a single one in his very small repertory that is in the least suitable for the new congregation; and for the first time in his life he finds himself called upon to stand alone with no one to consult, no one to lean on, no one to help him, and in so much a worse condition than the aforesaid Robinson Crusoe that the indigenous sons of the soil come and stare at him with an eye to their chances of getting a meal out of him, or making a meal off him, in the meantime doing, as the wicked always have done since the Psalmist's days, making mouths at him and ceasing not!

Talk of college dons being thrown away upon a handful of bumpkins! You forget that the cultured Academic has almost always some resources within himself, some tastes, some pursuits; and if he spends too many hours in his library, at any rate his time does not hang so very heavily upon his hands. When he goes among his people he will always have something to tell them which they did not know before, and something to inquire of them which they will be glad to tell him about. But your young city curate pitchforked into a rural benefice when all his sympathies and habits and training are of the streets streety, is the most forlorn, melancholy, and dazed of all human creatures. An omnibus driver compelled to keep a lighthouse could scarcely be more deserving of our commiseration. Ask him in his moments of candour and depression, when he realizes that he has reached the limit of his earthly hopes, when he has been in his parsonage long enough to know that he will never leave it for any other cure, when he realizes that he must (by the nature of the case, and by the unalterable law which prevails for such as he) wax poorer and poorer year by year, and that men may come and men may go, but he will stay where he is till he drops—ask him what he thinks of the bliss of a country living, its independence, its calm, its sweetness, its security, above all, ask him whether he does not think the great charm of his position is that he can never be turned out of it, and I think you will find some of these young fellows impatiently giving you just the answer you did *not* expect. I am sure you will find *some* among them who will reply: "It is a useful life for a time. It is a happy life for a time. For a time there is a joy in the country parson's life which no other life can offer; but we have come to see that this boasted fixity of tenure is the weak point, not the strong one; it is movement we want among us, not stagnation; the Parson's Freehold is a fraud."

Our vehement young friends in the first warmth of their conversion to new ideas are apt to express themselves with more force than elegance, and to push their elders somewhat rudely from behind. But they mean what they say, and I am glad they are coming to think as they do. As for us, the veterans who have lived through sixty summers and more, there is no cloud of promise for us in the horizon. *We* are not the men who have anything to gain by any change; we know the corner of the churchyards where our bones will lie. We do not delude ourselves; some of us never looked for any career when we retired into the wilderness. We asked for a refuge only, and that we have found.

Oh, Hope of all the ends of the earth, is it a small thing that for the remainder of our days we are permitted to witness for Thee among the poor and sad and lowly ones?

But you, the strong and young and fervid, take heed how you leave the life of the camp, its stir and throb and discipline, too soon. Take heed how before the time you join the reserve, only to discover too late that you are out of harmony with your surroundings, that you are fretting against the narrowness of the inclosure within which you are confined, that there is for you no outlook—none—only a bare subsistence and a safe berth, as there is for other hulks laid up to rot at ease. If that discovery comes upon you soon enough, break away! *Make* the change that will not come, and leave others to chuckle over their fixity of tenure, and their security, and their trumpery boast that "no one can turn them out." But let us have your testimony before we part—you and we. Bear witness Yes or No! Has the consciousness of occupying a position from which you could never be removed raised you in your own estimation, or helped you for one single moment to do your duty? Has it never kept you down? *Frauds* are for the weak, not for the strong—for the coward, not for the brave; they are for those who only live to rust at ease, as if to breathe were life; they are not for such as make the ventures of Faith, and help their brethren to overcome the world.

III.
THE CHURCH AND THE VILLAGES.

FEW men can have watched the movements of opinion during the last few years without being impressed by the change of attitude observable in the two contending parties engaged upon the assault and defence of the possessions of that mysterious entity which goes by the name of the Church of England.

This entity it must be premised, so far as it has a collective existence, exists in the person of certain officials who are supposed to be devoting their lives to certain duties, and are in the possession of funds which, after every deduction from the grossly exaggerated estimates of the rhetoricians, are certainly large, and yet are being added to every week by the lavish offerings of the English people. We must go back to a remote past if we desire to trace the origin of that reserve fund for the maintenance of our clergy on which they now live; a fund which has gone on growing, sometimes rapidly, sometimes slowly, for considerably more than a thousand years.

When people talk of *disendowing* the Church of England, they mean that this accumulated fund shall be confiscated by the nation for whose benefit it exists, and that it shall no longer be used for the purpose to which it has been so long devoted.

But what is this *Church* that it is to be despoiled and beggared, to be disestablished and disendowed? We cannot call it a corporation, for it has no corporate existence as a chartered company or a college has. It has no representatives in the Lower House of Parliament, as the universities have. It has no common council with disciplinary powers, as the Incorporated Society of Law or the Inns of Court have. It has no *voice* speaking with authority, no homogeneity deserving the name. It cannot pass ordinances for the regulation of its minutest affairs, or impose rules of conduct upon any one, or levy the smallest contribution from man, woman, or child by its own decrees. You may call it an army if you please; but it is an army in which the commissioned officers have no control over the rank and file, no power of enforcing attendance at drill, no articles of war which any one heeds, and no generals whom any one fears. This mysterious entity, which is the sum-total of a multitude of more or less isolated units, we say is the owner of lands and buildings and rent-charge, and this property it is said is the property of the Church—the Church? *Nos numerus sumus!*

Without any very great misuse of language, it may be said that among us there is another mysterious entity; this, too, the sum-total of a number of isolated units. These units, too, were only the other day in possession of houses and lands, and buildings considered to be public buildings; the units were almost in the same position as the clergy are at this moment, freeholders and practically irremovable; they were expected to perform certain duties which, as a rule, they performed with zeal and fidelity. In many cases, when sickness or old age came upon them, they discharged their functions by deputy; they had practically little or no discipline of control over them; "visitors" who never visited, feoffees who never interfered, governors who never governed. Each of these functionaries was called a Schoolmaster, and the building in which he officiated was called *a* school. The sum-total of these many units had no name; but if the public buildings were rightly called schools, the aggregate of them might for convenience be called *The School*. A noun of multitude, standing in the same relation to its units as the current term "the Church" does to its units—the Churches.

To whom did the property from which the schools were kept in efficiency, and their masters furnished with a maintenance— sometimes with much more than a mere maintenance—to whom did this property belong? I can find but one answer. It was the property of the nation; a reserve fund which the nation had permitted certain individuals to set apart from time to time for the furtherance of the education of the people, the object aimed at being considered so excellent that the conditions imposed upon posterity by the founders were allowed to remain in force, these founders being supposed to have entered into a contract with the nation that, in consideration of the value of the surrender made, the reserve of property should be sanctioned, and the conditions imposed be held to be binding upon posterity. The land or the rent-charges which yesterday were private possessions ceased to be so to-day: they *were* private property, they became public property, and constituted the Educational Reserve.

I can no longer resist the conviction that, as in the one case so in the other, the nation may reconsider its treaty with School or Church; may determine that the reserve hitherto set apart for the education of a class, or a district, or the founder's kin, should no longer be applied according to the compact sanctioned in previous ages, and may in the same way reconsider its compact with the alienation of property now known as Church property, and deal with that far larger reserve hitherto applied for the promotion of the moral and spiritual welfare of the people. The nation has the right to do this, as it undoubtedly has the power. Whether in this case *summum jus* would not be found to be *summa injuria* is quite another question.

But it is one thing to say this large reserve shall be administered otherwise than it is, and quite another thing to say that it shall cease to exist as a reserve at all. It is one thing to deal with our ecclesiastical endowments on the lines that school endowments have been dealt with, and quite another to deal with them as Henry the Eighth dealt with the property of the religious houses. To adopt the one course would be readjustment, to adopt the other would be confiscation. Nevertheless, if the majority of the new electorate should decidedly and unequivocally pronounce that such is its pleasure, assuredly the property now held in reserve in the shape of religious endowments will be confiscated. Religion will be the luxury of the rich and well-to-do; the proletariate and the agricultural labourer will have to supply themselves with an inferior article, or to do without it altogether.

If a revolution so tremendous, if a calamity so overwhelming, is to befall this nation, and is to take effect by the deliberate choice of its people, at least let a great nation address itself to the task with the semblance of dignity; at least let it be clearly explained and firmly adhered to that the clergy reserve is not to be given over to general pillage. Do not be guilty of the baseness of bidding for the votes of the proletariate by holding out hopes of a general scramble. Do not corrupt the poor dwellers in the villages by inviting them to embark in a filibustering raid upon their friends and neighbours.

*   *   *   *   *

It is a question which a philosopher might worthily employ himself in answering—how it has come to pass that during the last fifty years the struggle for supremacy between political parties has tended to become less and less a regular *warfare* and to assume more and more the character of a *game*. Nay! It is rapidly developing into a game rather more of chance than of skill, and one in which the most daring and reckless adventurer is just as likely to sweep off the stakes as the most gifted and sagacious player. It is one of the most unhappy results of this condition of affairs that there has grown up in our midst a class of touts and hangers-on who do the dirty work of either side and bring discredit upon both. They are the swell-mob of politics. Such creatures live by inventing grievances and fomenting discontent, their doctrine being that whatever is is wrong; their artillery is always charged with explosive promises. These men are going up and down the land loudly proclaiming that the parsons have robbed *the poor* of their own, and are holding out to their dupes the wildest hopes that when the spoliation comes *the poor* shall be the first to benefit by the great change.

We shall never be able to silence the voice of charlatans. The sausage-seller in Aristophanes is the type of a class of men who have found no scope for their talents in any honest calling, and who because they must live have been forced into the trade of lying vociferously. I do not write for these—to these I have no word to say. It is with the men whose hearts are throbbing with some patriotism, and who have not lost all loyalty to truth and honour, that I desire to have my dealings. It is with such that I would humbly and earnestly expostulate, whatever their philosophical or political opinions, and whatever may be their creed. Even if it were as easy to prove, as it is demonstrably the reverse, that there ever did exist in England at any time or in any place a right on the part of the poor to any portion of the tithes of a parish or to the glebe, who, it may be asked, are *the poor*? The receivers of parochial relief, whether in the work-house or outside it? Or every able-bodied peasant who claims to belong to the needy classes? Are you going to ask the agricultural labourer to cry for spoliation, and to bribe him to raise the cry by the promise of converting him into what our fathers called a "sturdy beggar"? And then are there no poor artisans? Are the millions of our towns to be left out in the cold while Hodge disports himself with his new possessions? Are Liverpool and East London to go on as they are, while Little Mudborough is to enjoy a feast of fat things?

But the demagogues who live to corrupt the people have promises to make to others than the labourers. They are telling the tenant-farmers, too, that they will be gainers by the great confiscation, and endeavouring to persuade them, too, that when it comes they will be relieved from the burden of the tithes. Would they be so? If the payment of tithe were abolished to-morrow, can any sane man believe that the tenant-farmer would be allowed to put the tithe into his pocket or to keep it there? Can any sane man believe that rents would not rise exactly in proportion to the amount of charges from which the tenant was relieved? Rent is nothing more than the money payment supposed to represent the just return which the owner claims from the occupier for the privilege of cultivating his land. The occupier makes his account and calculates how much he can gain by the compact. The landlord's share is his rent. He is the sleeping partner. Relieve the expenses of the going concern from the payment of the tithe, or, which is the same thing, add it to the profits, and what power on earth will prevent the landlord, directly or indirectly, sooner or later, absorbing the proceeds of the newly-created *bonus*?

Moreover, if you begin to "do away with the tithes," are you going to do away with them *only* in the case where the parson receives them and does something—at any rate *some*thing—in return for the income he derives from them? Are you going to let the tithes be levied as before where they are paid to laymen, to corporations, or colleges? Are those tithes which are necessarily spent in the parish by the resident parson to be "done away with," but all such tithes as are necessarily carried out of the parish and paid to a London company, an alien, or a college at Oxford or Cambridge, to be levied as before? Is it a *gravamen* against the parson that he spends his tithe where it is paid him, and among the people who pay it, and that he is bound in return for it to do the payers some services which they may exact on demand? Are you going to confiscate the tithe where the receiver does something for it, and to let the man who does nothing for it collect it as before? Imagine the amazement and disgust of a farmer who should be told that his neighbour on the other side of the hedge is never to pay tithe again because in that parish there has been a parson to pillage; but that he, on this side of the hedge, is to pay it as before, because Mr. Tomkins, or Mrs. John Smith, or the Saddlers' Company is the lay impropriator, and the rights of property are to be respected. It would not be long, I imagine, before our friend the farmer would go for the lay impropriator, and with a will too.

But, if the labourer and the tenant-farmer are not to be cajoled by promises that must needs be illusory, least of all are the landlords to be gained over by the inducement held out to them that they, of all men, are to benefit by the change. They more than any other class are responsible for the loud outcry that has been raised. The tithe-rent-charge is a first charge upon the produce of the land. They are the landlords who, as a class, have done their best to make people forget this fact. How often have we heard of a landlord or his agent declaring loudly, "I have nothing to do with the tithe—that is a matter between the tenant and the parson!" A more monstrous assertion it would be difficult to invent! Far more true would be the direct opposite, if the parson, or the impropriator, should say, "I, as receiver of tithe, have nothing to do with you, the tenant—the tithe is no concern of yours; my claim is upon the owner of the soil!" In point of fact, it is in the last resort upon the landlord, and the landlord alone, that the tithe-owner, lay or clerical, has his claim.

*   *   *   *   *

But, if we should only aggravate the incidence of the immense calamity which would ensue from the confiscation of the clergy reserve by handing over the spoils to the labourers, or the proletariate, or the farmers, or the landlords, and yet the electorate should resolve to carry out this great spoliation, and call upon the executive to sweep away the clerical incomes, and lay its hand upon the property from which these incomes are derived; what is to be done with this huge fund so confiscated, and how are we to prevent the landlords being in some form or other the only gainers by the change?

If confiscation comes, let it come, say I, as no half-measure. Let there be no bargaining, no tinkering, no compromise—in fact, no mercy! No—no mercy! Let this thing be done in root-and-branch fashion. Let the nation set its face like a flint; let the Church—it would be the Church then—begin its new life naked and bare. Both sides will have a bad time of it. It takes little to decide which will have the worst time of it, the starved Church or the starved people.

Set the two forces foot to foot,
And every man knows who'll be winner,
Whose faith in God has e'er a root
That goes down deeper than his dinner.

Therefore, if indeed this nation decides that it can do without religious teachers, and that these shall live of those who want them, let us put up our parish churches to auction, and dispose of the glebes to the highest bidder, and flood the market with comfortable parsonage-houses, sold without reserve, and let the tithe be levied by the tax-gatherer, and let *it be levied from the owner of the soil*, as the land-tax is. Furthermore, let us have no assignment of any share of the plunder to any class or any special fund. Let us hand over the proceeds of the sale of churches and houses and lands to the Commissioners for the Extinguishing of the National Debt, and not to the ratepayers, not to the Education Commissioners, nor to the Commissioners in Lunacy for building madhouses, or any other cheerful and heroic object. Let us have a measure which shall be simple and thorough, with the fewest possible details to vex and embarrass us all. As the parsons die, sell their houses, their glebes and their churches, and let the State at once appropriate the tithe. Let us be brought face to face with the real meaning of a revolution, the tremendous magnitude of which few men can have the faintest conception of. In less than a year after the measure had become law, we should begin to know in what an experiment we had embarked. The sooner our eyes were opened the better for us all. The logic of facts is better than gabble.

Nevertheless, firmly convinced as I am that such a revolution would be an immeasurable calamity to the people of this country, and especially so to the agricultural districts, I am quite as firmly convinced that the present condition of affairs as regards the tenure and administration of the property now constituting the clergy reserves cannot possibly go on much longer; that the mere mockery and pretence of discipline among the clergy themselves must be replaced by something much more real and effective; that, in short, some large and radical measures of Church reform are being called for, such as the nation feels must and shall be carried out, though the great body of the people do not yet see, and cannot yet be expected to see, on what fundamental principles such reform should be advocated, or on what lines such reform should travel.

As a preliminary, as a *sine quâ non* of all really effective Church reform, it seems to me that, first and foremost, you must begin, not by *disestablishing*, but by *establishing*, the Church. As things are among us, it seems to me that the very word establishment is a confession on the part of those who use it that they have failed to discover the right word for that which they would fain obliterate.

We say the Church is a great landlord and wealthy owner of property. Ought not such an owner to have some control over its own and some voice in the disposition of that property. Every railroad company in the land, every joint-stock bank or co-operative association for the providing of milk and butter, every society for the protection of cats and dogs, has a constitution. It has its directors or governors, its recognized officers, its power to make or to alter at least its own bye-laws, its liberty to dispose of its own funds within certain limits, the privilege of meeting and of discussing its own affairs when and where it pleases, and the right of applying to the Legislature of the country for larger powers if such shall appear necessary for the carrying out of objects not dreamt of at its first start.

The Church is absolutely lacking in all these respects, for the very simple reason that the Church, viewed as a going concern in possession of property, has nothing that can be called a constitution.

* * * * *

If the glaring anomalies and the wholly unjustifiable grotesqueness which startle us at every turn when we begin to discuss "Church questions" are to be removed, where are we to begin, and what should be the lines on which any scheme of readjustment should proceed?

First and foremost, let all obsolete and antiquated privileges, which are survivals of a long extinct condition of affairs, be swept away, and with the privileges let the disabilities go also. Let no man be made either more or less than a citizen of the Empire by reason of his being in any sense a member of the Church—not a peer of the realm on the one hand, not disqualified from entering the House of Commons on the other.

As a preliminary to giving the Church a working constitution, it is my conviction that the bishops should no longer have seats in the House of Lords. I cannot see how any director or overseer of any corporation, or indeed of any department of the State, should be made a peer of the realm by virtue of his holding office. I am not wholly ignorant of our constitutional history, although into the historical aspect of the question I decline to enter now. The facts are what we have to face; and as things are, however much we may deplore it, there seems just as little reason why bishops should be raised to the peerage as why the naval lords of the Admiralty should be created barons. But, if you dismiss the bishops from the Upper House, you certainly cannot exclude the inferior clergy from the lower one. Whether in the one case the Church or the House of Lords would be much the loser may very reasonably be doubted, notwithstanding the conspicuous ability which is and has for long been characteristic of the Episcopal Bench. In the other case, the Church and the House of Commons are just as little likely to be much the gainers by letting clergymen represent the constituencies in Parliament. As in France, so would it be in England; the clerical candidates would be very few, the clerical members fewer. That, however, does not affect the question whether or not clerical disabilities should be abolished.

But by far the most necessary and radical reform that is imperatively called for is the abolition of that preposterous antiquarian curiosity, the Parson's Freehold.

The philosopher of the future who "with larger, other eyes than ours," shall survey the history of our institutions and tell of their origin, their growth or their decay, will, I believe, be amazed and perplexed by nothing so much as by the strange vitality of this legal phenomenon—the *Parson's Freehold*. That any man who is in any sense a public servant should, by virtue of being nominated to hold an office, be made tenant for life of a real estate from which only by an act of his own can he be removed—*that* would seem to most of us so entirely startling and outrageous in the abstract as to be absolutely intolerable in the concrete reality. Let us look this thing in the face.

Imagine a postman or a prime minister, a clerk in the Custom House or the captain of a man-of-war, an assistant in a draper's shop or your own gardener, having an estate for life in his office, and being able to draw his pay to his dying day, though he might be for years blind and deaf and paralyzed and imbecile—so incapable, in fact, that he could not even appoint his own deputy, or so indifferent that he cared not whether there was any deputy to discharge the duties which he himself was paid to perform. Imagine any public servant being thrown into prison for a flagrant misdemeanour, or worse than a misdemeanour, and coming back to his work when the term of his imprisonment was over, receiving the arrears of pay which had accrued during the time he was in gaol, and quietly settling down into the old groove as if nothing had happened. Imagine *any* public servant being suspended from his office for habitual drunkenness, suspended say for two years, and not even requiring to be reinstated when the two years were over, but gaily taking his old seat and returning to his desk and his bottle, as irremovable from the emoluments of the first as he was inseparable from his devotion to the last.

Yet all this, and much more than this, is possible for us beneficed clergymen. I am myself the patron of a benefice from which the late rector was nonresident for fifty-three years. Is it at all conceivable that we should continue to keep up this condition of affairs under which we have been living so long? The last thing that any other public servant would dare to confess would be that he was physically or intellectually or morally unfit for his office. The retort in his case would be obvious enough—then leave it, and make way for a better man. But the holder of the Parson's Freehold smilingly replies, "Certainly I will retain my hold upon the income after paying my deputy. Am I not a landlord? and as tenant for life I will assuredly cling to my own."

Being such as we are, men of flesh and blood as others, and occupying the frightfully impregnable position which we do; fenced about with all sorts of legal safeguards which put us above our parishioners on the one hand, and out of the reach of our bishops on the other; having, as we have, an almost unlimited power of turning our benefices into sinecures while we reside upon them, or of leaving them to the veriest hireling to serve while we are disporting ourselves in foreign travel almost as long as we should choose to stay away;—I know no more splendid testimony to the high and honourable character of the English clergy than that which would be wrung from their worst enemies who should fairly consider what the law of the land would allow of their being if they were so disposed—and what, in fact, they are. It is because as a class they are so animated by a high ideal; because as a class their conscience is their law; it is, therefore, that, in spite of legal safeguards which in their tendency are corrupting and demoralizing, as a class they are incomparably *better than they need be.* The clergy of the

Church of England constitute the one protected interest in the universe that does not languish. Nevertheless, *C'est magnifique, mais ce n'est pas la guerre.* These things ought not so to be.

*   *   *   *   *

How then are the evils inseparable from the present state of things to be remedied? They are evils which do not appear on the surface where the clergy themselves are conscientious, high-minded, and zealous, throwing themselves into their duties with self-denying earnestness, and hardly aware of how much they might abuse their powers if they were so disposed. They are very real and scandalous evils in the case of the careless, the worthless, and the immoral; that is, exactly in the case of those whom we can least afford to leave as they are.

I can see no other plan for utilizing to the utmost the resources already at our disposal than by sweeping away altogether this archaic anomaly of the parson's freehold. We are all a great deal too tenacious of vested rights, a great deal too reluctant to deal harshly with those who have accepted any office under certain conditions expressed or implied, to allow of our disturbing the present occupants of the benefices, or to bring them under any new *régime*. As long as the existing beneficed clergy choose to retain their hold upon their benefices, obviously they must be left undisturbed; as they are freeholders, so they must continue to be, and practically irremovable; but, as they drop off either by death or voluntary resignation, let the freehold be vested in other hands. Let us follow the main lines upon which the Endowed School Commissioners pursued their revolution in the case of the educational reserve fund, learning experience by their blunders, their failures or their *fads*.

And when we do so, where shall we find ourselves?

1. The freehold of every church, churchyard, glebe-house and lands, together with the tithes and any other invested funds now constituting the endowment of a benefice, would be vested in a body of trustees or governors exactly as the estates and buildings of the endowed schools are at this moment. These governors would have the administration of this estate entrusted to them, and be personally and collectively responsible for its management—responsible, that is, to a *duly constituted authority* with a power of enforcing its precepts.

- 73 -

2. All liability to keep house and chancel in repair, together with all powers of mortgaging the lands of a benefice, would be transferred from the incumbent to the governing body of trustees.

3. The patronage of every benefice would, as a matter of course, pass out of the hands of the present patrons, and would be vested in the trustees of the benefice; exactly as the patronage of Shrewsbury and Sedbergh schools passed out of the hands of St. John's College, Cambridge, or as the patronage of Thame school passed out of the hands of New College, Oxford, or as the patronage of Brentwood, Kirkleatham, and Bosworth schools has passed out of the hands of *private patrons* into those of the newly-constituted governing bodies.

4. The governors in presenting to a benefice would in each case be expected to consider the financial position in which it happened to be at the time of the vacancy, and would be empowered to determine what amount of net income could be assigned to the incumbent according to the circumstances of the estate in their hands; in all cases guaranteeing a minimum stipend and, in cases where a house was provided, a house free of all rates, taxes, and repairs.

5. The governing body would be required to render an account of all moneys received and expended to the *constituted authority*, to which they would be answerable.

6. Any clergyman presented to a benefice by the governing body would be liable to be dismissed for inefficiency or misconduct; such dismissal to be subject to an appeal as against caprice, malevolence, or tyranny.

* * * * *

Before proceeding further, it will be as well at this point to consider an objection that may be offered, and then to see how such a reform as that proposed would work.

First, with regard to handing over the property of a benefice, together with the patronage, to a body of trustees. Such a course will certainly be denounced as revolutionary, and of course that word has a very alarming sound. But I venture to remind objectors that we have already embarked upon this revolutionary course, and on a very large scale too. We have already taken vast estates out of the hands of ecclesiastical corporations, and vested them in the hands of the

Ecclesiastical Commissioners. We have already made our bishops stipendiaries, receiving their *salaries* from the holders of their estates; and happy are those deans and canons who are in such a case, and not in the pitiable condition of landlords with their farms upon their hands, or let to tenants who, just now, can make their own terms with the panic-stricken lifeholders of the freehold. But this is not all. There are at least a thousand benefices in England at this moment, the patronage of which *is already in the hands of trustees*; and in many of these cases—in many more cases than people suspect—the very freehold of the church itself is vested in those trustees, who have almost entire control over the funds, and almost entire control over the fabric of the church. At this moment, as I write, there is lying on my table an application from *the Trustees* of St. Excellent's Church, at Jericho, asking me to subscribe for the erection of a tower, and pleading that the *Trustees* have done all that was possible, and have been loyally *seconded* by their devoted vicar.

Ask those who know anything of what has been going on in the second city in England during the last forty years what condition the masses at Liverpool would be in at this moment but for the church-building on the Trustee system which has been in operation there so long. Ask them whether that system has worked well or ill, and whether there is any reason to regret that the patronage of the Trustee churches is not in other hands.

*   *   *   *   *

And now with regard to the working of the scheme proposed.

The rectory of Claylump finds itself vacant by the promotion of its rector to the bishopric of Loo Choo. The governors forthwith proceed to take a survey of the property they hold in trust, and to look about for a new parson. The character and qualification of the various candidates for the vacant benefice are carefully inquired into, and, the choice being made, the new incumbent is presented to the bishop of the see and instituted with all fitting and necessary solemnity.

But before he enters upon his charge the new rector has been informed that, in view of the governors being responsible for certain outgoings, they can for the present guarantee the parson only a minimum income of x pounds per annum, to be increased according as the funds at their disposal shall allow of the augmentation.

Observe that we already find ourselves face to face with the problem which has been found so difficult of solution—viz., how to deal with Ecclesiastical Dilapidations. A beneficed clergyman at present may, if he pleases, let his house tumble about his ears—may let his barn be tenanted by the rats, turn his stable into a pigsty, and, keeping his glebe in his own hands, render it valueless for his successor for the next five years. At his death he may be absolutely insolvent. The next incumbent is, however, called upon to put all into tenantable repair at his own cost, and by the very fact of accepting the living is liable for these substantial repairs.

Or a beneficed clergyman may do exactly the reverse. Being tenant for life of a living of less than three hundred a year, he may convert the parsonage-house into a noble mansion—erect hot-houses and conservatories *ad libitum*, build stables for a dozen horses, and lay out acres of the glebe in ornamental gardens; and he too may die in difficulties. At the avoidance of the living the bishop may give orders for pulling down half the house and more than half the appurtenances; but the question of who is to pay for the expenses of the alteration will present a serious difficulty, and may be settled in the strangest way at last. As long as the living is in a good neighbourhood, with certain advantages which it is unnecessary to particularise, it will not be hard to find another man of fortune who for the sake of the house will consent to accept the cure. But, if it chance that a neighbourhood has "changed," and the parish has become otherwise than a desirable place of residence, that parish may find it very hard indeed to get any who will face the terrible prospect of having to keep up a palace on £300 a year. In either case—that of finding himself with a tumble-down rectory, or that of finding himself with an entirely unsuitable one—the incoming parson will assuredly have to make his account to submit to a serious abatement from the nominal revenue of his preferment, and will assuredly be in no better position than he would be if, not he, but the trustees, were the owners of the parson's freehold.

But once more. Let us suppose that the new rector under the new *régime* finds it desirable to add to his parsonage-house for any reason or for none. What follows? Is he to be allowed to do as he pleases? Certainly not. If he can get the consent of his governors, well and good; without that consent he would have no more right to build up than to pull down. He would be living in an *official residence* provided for him. Clearly, he could not be permitted to deal with it as if it were his own.

Again, let us suppose that the parsonage should sorely need repair, and that the parson, being poor or otherwise unwilling to be meddled with, should declare it was good enough for him. Would it be reasonable to let an obstructive eccentric continue living in a house which was seriously lessening in value from the want of structural repairs? It is obvious that the governors who were liable for these repairs being duly executed, and whose interest was to maintain the buildings in good and tenantable condition, would interpose. The official residence having to be kept up by the income of the benefice in their view would clearly not be regarded as something to be handed over in its entirety to the present holder of the living, as if his personal interest were the only thing to consider.

As it would not be allowable for a Plutus to over-build, so it would not be permitted to a niggard to let the parsonage fall into disrepair. In either case the governing body would have a voice, and over the buildings of the benefice they would exercise a general supervision and control.

What, however, will startle most people, and especially clergymen, is the proposal to give to *any* body at all or any person or any officer the power to dismiss a parson from his cure. Yet, as an abstract question, why should the parson be the only functionary to enjoy the immunity he does? Is it because it does not matter much to his parishioners whether he is fit or unfit, moral or immoral, active or indolent, whether he is exhibiting an example of holiness or is a mere helot whose daily walk is an abominable scandal? As things are, the more conscientious a clergyman is, the more easily you may hunt him out of his preferment; such men cannot bear to stay where— as they put it in all earnestness and devout sincerity—they are "doing no good." Such men are ready enough to go out into the wilderness if you tell them they are not wanted or are hindering Christ's work by staying where they are. But tell the bad man that he is not wanted in his parish, and his ministrations are hateful to the people among whom he lives, and he will laugh in your face with the grim joke that, if the people don't like to come to church, they may stay away, and if they don't want him at the font or the altar or the grave, so much the better; he will have less work to do for his money. The thick-skinned with a seared conscience defies you; safe in the possession of the parson's freehold, he holds his own.

How is it that we are always so ready to conjure up the worst imaginable evils when any new proposal is offered to us, and always draw some picture of abuses and horrors when we begin to think of any great change, as if there were no abuses and horrors which called for the change? "A body of governors with a power of dismissal," it is said; "why, no man's position would be safe!" To begin with, I do not see why the first thing to be aimed at should be that *any one's* position should be *safe*. The first thing that is needed, imperatively needed, is that the duties of any office, from that of the Prime Minister downwards, should be effectively discharged. It may be very desirable that the driver of an express train should be safe of getting his wages as long as he lives. It is infinitely more desirable that the train itself should not run off the metals from the aforesaid driver going to sleep.

But *whose* position in the case before us would be *unsafe*? As a rule, only his whose position ought to be unsafe. The Endowed Schools Commissioners have been at work for more than twenty years. Every one of their schemes gives to the governing body a power of dismissal, and that too with usually no appeal. During these twenty years, I have never heard of more than two cases in which this power has been exercised; so slow are we Englishmen to be hard on an old servant, or to use to the utmost the powers which we have in our hand.

*   *   *   *   *

Our next point to consider is, what should be the constitution of the governing body?

Let it be premised that, in embarking upon a reform so radical as this that is contemplated, I for one at the outset shrink from committing ourselves to any details until we have first laid down the grand principles on which we are going to proceed. Moreover, it must never be forgotten that the circumstances of every parish or district in England vary to an extent which they who have never thought much upon the subject could hardly bring themselves to believe. In a matter of so much intricacy and complexity we must not be afraid to feel our way, and at any rate let us have at the outset as few hard-and-fast lines as may be.

With this caution and proviso, I yet venture to suggest that the main lines to be laid down should be as follows:—

1. The governing body should not be too large, nor should it ever be chosen from the inhabitants of the parish exclusively.

2. It should be a representative body.

3. Its meetings should not be held too frequently.

4. Its proceedings should be duly chronicled, and a record kept which might be produced and referred to when necessary.

*   *   *   *   *

1. Not too large, because experience proves that any administrative body is in danger of becoming a speechifying body, and liable to be influenced by pressure from without, almost exactly in proportion to the increase of its numbers. Nor should this body be chosen exclusively from the inhabitants of the parish. In the case of small parishes, it would be quite impossible to find persons qualified to exercise the powers to be conferred, or fitted by education and intelligence to occupy the independent and important position of governor.

2. It will be necessary that the governing body should in all cases be a representative body. In such a body what interests should be represented?

(i) First the owners of the land on which tithes are paid. Observe, I do not say the tithe-*payers*; for, of all the objectionable practices which have sprung up among us affecting the tenure of the land, and the burdens it has to bear, none appears to me more mischievous or indefensible, none has done more to make the tillers of the soil discontented, or led them more passionately to set themselves against their best friends, than the practice sanctioned by the Legislature of calling upon the tenant to pay the tithe in addition to the rent of his land. As long as this goes on, so long will both tenant and landlord be tempted to make common cause with one another in hopes of getting rid of the tithe. You might just as well call upon the tenant to pay the landlord's mortgage interest, or the jointures and annuities with which the estate is charged, or the premiums upon his policies of insurance, as call upon him to pay the tithe. A landlord holds his lands subject to certain charges, which are antecedent to any profits that may remain to him after they are discharged.

The land-tax, the county-rates, the tithe, are all on the same level; so are the jointures, annuities, and interest of money borrowed. Of course the landlord would gladly throw them all upon the tenant if he could, and does throw upon him all he can. In permitting him to follow this course, you tempt the tenant to cry out, "Away with this payment, and away with that!" and you tempt the landlord to cry, "Amen! So be it, as long as my rent is assured me!" Worried by the annual recurrence of *extra* payments, for which he has to provide at all sorts of inconvenient times, the tenant is ready enough to demand relief from these burdens, never reflecting that he is playing the landlord's game, directly or indirectly robbing somebody else to enrich the owner of the soil. "Down with the rates!" means "Throw them upon the Consolidated Fund and let the taxpayer relieve the landlord." "Down with the jointures!" would mean "Rob the dowagers and let the landlord be the richer for the pillage." "Down with the mortgage interest!" would mean "Up with the debtor at the expense of the creditor;" and "Down with the tithe!" would mean the extinction of the parson, but with the gain of not a shilling ultimately to the tenant, though with a very considerable gain to the owner of the land. It must be, and it is, demoralizing to allow the payment of the tithe to be regarded as an *extra* with which the tenant is chargeable. The obligation to pay the tithe is a condition antecedent to the *owner* of the soil enjoying the very possession of his land. The tithe is a *rent-charge* upon the land, exactly as an annuity or jointure is—or, if you choose to call it a tax because the term tax is an odious word, and therefore serviceable when you want to make those you hate odious—it is a landlord's *tax*, and no tenant should be allowed to pay it without having the right under all circumstances of deducting it from his rent.

Moreover, without yielding to the temptation of straying into an historical argument, yet remembering that in the past there was a very close connection between the landlord whose estate supplied the tithe from which the parson was supported and the patron of the living to which the parson was instituted, I think there are good reasons why the owners of the soil liable to pay tithe should be represented in the proposed governing body of a benefice. Where the parish was a close parish—*i.e.*, owned by a single landlord—he would naturally and very properly be the only person eligible, or at any rate capable of nominating the tithe-owner's representative. Where there were many landlords, they could elect their representatives—one or more, as the case might be—in the ordinary way.

(ii) As the owners of land subject to the payment of tithes should be represented, so should the ratepayers of the parish have their representative upon the board of governors. And here I confess I cannot see that you could introduce any religious test whereby any one should be disqualified by reason of his creed. I do not believe that in ordinary cases any real inconveniences would arise. That under no circumstances conceivable evils should emerge is too much to hope for; but whether or not, we must, I repeat, face the facts, and what reasonable man, who watches the signs of the times, will be sanguine enough to expect that, in our days, we have any chance of extorting from the Legislature anything in the shape of a conscience clause? But, when I speak of ratepayers, I mean *bonâ fide* payers of rates. I exclude from this category the compound householder: I by no means exclude unmarried women who pay their own rates and taxes, who are often among the most sagacious, high-minded, and exemplary inhabitants of a country parish, or of a town one too, for that matter. If any should have a voice in the choice of a representative governor, clearly they should.

(iii) But, if the owners of the soil and the ratepayers should be represented, it would be more than unreasonable—it would be a monstrous injustice—that the regular worshippers in the church should be left without their representative governors. I am quite aware that some people are ready with all sorts of difficulties and all sorts of objections when we come to deal with the qualification of church membership, and quite aware, too, that at this point one is sorely tempted to do that which I protested against above—viz., go into details; but I resist the temptation, simply expressing my conviction that there *can* be and there is no real and insuperable difficulty in defining what is meant by "regular worshippers," and that such difficulty would vanish at once if we were really in earnest in grappling with it. I am not hinting at a compromise. Here as elsewhere what we want is—common sense!

(iv) Again, I conceive that on any board of governors there should be a representative appointed by the bishop of the diocese, and that he should be a resident in the archdeaconry in which the benefice was situated. In every board of directors, be it of a railway or bank or insurance company, it is held to be essential to effectiveness that one or more of such directors should have some pretension to technical or professional knowledge of the business carried on. Is it too much to ask that at least one *expert* should be found upon every body of church governors? Such a representative would, if discreet and able, be always listened to with respectful attention; if inclined to be domineering or impracticable, he would assuredly be outvoted when it came to a contest. He would be a voice, but he would be no more.

(v) It is conceivable, nay it is probable, that in addition to these representative governors it might in some cases be advisable that other members should be added to the governing body. Thus it might be contended by the present patrons of benefices, whether lay or clerical, that they should be represented, and I can see no particular objection to such a claim being allowed. It is also conceivable and probable that, after due consideration and discussion, it might be thought advisable to group two or more benefices together and vest their funds in the same body of governors. Indeed, in many country districts, where the endowments are very small and the population very sparse, it might prove extremely difficult and sometimes extremely undesirable to have a board of governors for each of these tiny units, let alone the absurd waste of power which in such cases would be inevitable. But, such as I have sketched it out, such in the main would be the constitution of the governing body of every benefice in the country, and to that governing body the freehold of that benefice and its appurtenances, together with the patronage thereof, should be handed over.

(vi) With regard to the qualification of those eligible for a seat upon the governing body, I am not prepared to discuss that question at the present stage. This, however, I know—viz., that there is only one subject of the Queen who is now disqualified from presenting a clergyman to any benefice in England. A Jew or a Mormonite, a Mohammedan or a Parsee, Mr. Bradlaugh or Mr. Congreve, may be, and for ought I know is, patron of the richest or the poorest living in England; but if any of these worthy persons should suddenly become influenced by Cardinal Manning and be received as a member of the Church of Rome, then and then only would he become incapable by law from exercising his patronage—then and then only would it pass out of his hands. If we have come to this pass, that in anything like a large majority of cases Churchmen should find themselves outvoted by Jews, Turks, infidels, and heretics in the governing bodies, would it not be pretty clear that something was wrong?

But would the functions of the governing body be confined to the management of the estate of a benefice and to the appointing and, where necessary, to the dismissal of the incumbent? Yes. It seems to me that the functions of a governing body should go no further. That was a golden rule which Lord Palmerston laid down for the governing bodies of our endowed schools, and which these bodies have generally had the wisdom to carry out in practice—"Get the best man you can find and—get out of his way!" It should be no part of the duties of the governing body to interfere with what may be called the internal affairs of the church and the ministrations of the parson. These should be matters of arrangement between the congregation and their minister. Let the powers and the duties of churchwardens be defined as clearly as may be—let the number of the churchwardens be increased if you will, or let the old *sidesman* be revived; but let it be clearly understood that the parish is one thing and the congregation is another. Let it be understood that the rector of the *parish* as a parish officer should be accountable to the governors in so far as they are trustees for the *parish* reserve fund; but in matters with which only the congregation worshipping habitually in the church are concerned, let no outsider have any *locus standi*. If in his administrations a clergyman insists on doing or leaving undone certain practices which are hateful to the congregation to which he ministers; if between priest and people things should come to a deadlock; by all means let it be allowable, as it ought to be, for the people to demand redress, and let them ask for that redress with authority and a claim to have their grievances considered. In such cases there would be no need of rushing into the law courts, no spiteful resort to costly legislation to crush or ruin a foolish, obstinate, and ignorantly conscientious clergyman. The congregation—speaking through their representatives, the churchwardens, sidesmen, or whatever other name you might choose to call them by— would lay their complaint before the bishop first, and as an ultimate resort would go to the governing body, and claim that their parson should be dismissed, on grounds which should be, of course, properly formulated.

And this brings us to another matter—viz., the prominence (I do not say pre-eminence) to be given to the congregational element in any readjustment of church regimen at the present time. It is idle to talk as if the Church were co-extensive with the nation, or as if the inhabitants of a parish were all worshippers in the church fabric. If a man now does not like the ritual or the doctrine offered to him in his parish church, he leaves it, and goes where he finds what he wants. It will always be so. There was a good deal of nonconformity in the Apostolic times, and there will be nonconformity as long as men love to have things their own way. If an apostle were to find himself rector of any parish in England, with an angel to play the organ, and a multitude of the heavenly host to chant the psalms and "render" the anthems, would Jannes and Jambres be satisfied? On the other hand, though it is impossible but that offences should arise (which means that offence should be *taken*), it is our duty and our interest to minimise the occasion of offence; and it is clearly neither right nor politic that any man should occupy such a position as that he may, if he please, go very far towards making himself a "lord over God's heritage," and by adopting such a course not only lessen his own influence, but commit a serious wrong to the assembly of worshippers to whom, after all, it must be remembered, he is appointed to minister, not to be an irresponsible dictator.

Wherever there is a "congregation of faithful men" regularly worshipping together in any church, the very sign and evidence of life among them is that there is a great deal of mere *business* to be got through. There are large sums of money raised for various purposes, there are organizations great and small to be looked to, there are meetings to be held, arrangements of very different kinds to be made, and work of all sorts to be done. It *must* be done, and it can *only* be done by the incumbent in conjunction and co-operation with the congregation; as long as the two work together all goes on smoothly, if they are at variance friction ensues. It would be preposterous that all the money collected by and through the voluntary contributions and the voluntary exertions of the congregation should be handed over to an outside body such as the governing body we have been dealing with above. Indeed, such a proposal scarcely deserves to be seriously considered; the congregation as a congregation must in all reason be allowed to manage its own affairs. But, inasmuch as no institution in the world can hope to flourish if its manager prove himself incompetent, quarrelsome, and fractious, and when it becomes apparent that the well-being of the institution is being sacrificed only to keep the wrong man in the wrong place, then you get rid of that wrong man, sometimes with joy, sometimes with sorrow. So should it be with our churches. To give the congregations the appointment of their parsons or to arm them with a veto would be to follow a course which all our experience warns us against, and to which—I cannot explain why—all our national habits of thought, convictions, and prejudices are opposed. But, under any circumstances, cases might occur where a reluctant congregation might find itself saddled with a minister who, after a fair trial, should prove himself altogether unsuited to deal with the peculiar conditions, social, financial, or religious—which presented themselves; and where such cases did occur the congregation in its own interests—to go no further—ought to have the opportunity of making its wishes or its objections known. As to graver matters, where a parson's moral character was in question, I do not think it worth while to deal with them. As to the proposal of setting up parochial councils in our country villages, I find it very hard to believe that this can have ever been put forward seriously by any sane man of the world. Surely, surely it can only be the clumsy joke of a dreamer which suggests that we should establish village parliaments for the discussion of matters of ritual and theology among the representatives of a population which sometimes counts by tens, usually by a few hundreds, and very rarely by thousands. In the single diocese of Norwich there are actually one hundred and two parishes in each of which the population is less than a hundred, including the last baby. Think of a parochial council in the parish of Bittering Parva, where I was once told "there are *between* fourteen and fifteen inhabitants!"

*   *   *   *   *

I am quite aware that the questions which still remain to be dealt with in considering any comprehensive measure of what is known as Church Reform are many and difficult, and some of them are of the highest importance. They will come on for discussion, we may be sure, and abler men than I am, and men better qualified to handle such questions, will doubtless engage in them.

In the hands of such men I would gladly leave the serious and difficult problems which are calling so loudly for solution. The power of dismissal of a parson from his cure, for other than moral offences, at once brings us face to face with the question, "How are we to provide for aged and broken-down clergy in their time of need?" It also suggests the question, "In what relations will the governing body stand to the congregation on the one side and the bishop on the other?" The throwing open the benefices to what is sure to be stigmatized as *open competition* will be distasteful to some, but will result in changes which I am convinced will be, on the whole, of immense benefit to clergy and people, and especially they will tend towards the promotion of the best men to the most valuable cures. Yet here too, when we come to details, it will be necessary to open our eyes to some difficulties, from which, however, we need not shrink, nor will they, I believe, be found so insuperable as may be imagined.

The training, too, of the younger clergy during their term of *apprenticeship*, if I may use the expression, and the general supervision and periodical inspection of the benefices which has now become the emptiest of forms, will assuredly be called for by all who desire a coherent scheme for the readjustment of matters ecclesiastical. It is hardly to be expected that we should be allowed to go on much longer in the rambling way we do.

If it were only the supremacy of this or that form of doctrine or worship, however dear to us, however sacred, that was at stake, I for one would not willingly embark in the conflict that is before us, or step out from the limits of the humble sphere in which I find myself. I would hold my peace except among my people, and try my best to till the little plot in the heritage of God which His good providence has assigned to me for my daily work. But there is much more at stake than any merely sectarian view of the case would have us believe. It is no mere fight between religious factions and sects and creeds. The question now is whether or not that machinery whereby the schooling of our moral sentiments has been carried on for ages shall be cast from us as a thing of nought, while we surrender ourselves to the private-venture teachers to provide a new machinery by-and-by. Are we to have no functionaries whose remonstrances any one need attend to? Is there to be no voice speaking with the semblance of authority, bidding the people do the right and avoid the evil? Is there to be no national worship, no national religion, and of course no national creed? How long can Christian ethics be supposed to last?

For ages the vessel of the State has gone on its way riding through a thousand storms, and buffeted by a million billows; its rudder has been at times unskilfully handled; at times the course has been set with evil consequences; at times the steersmen have been rash or blind. But shall we now, in an outbreak of passion or panic, unship that rudder and cut ourselves adrift, with never a helm to trust to, in the open sea?

IV.
QUIS CUSTODIET?

THERE are very few Societies started in our time which have done so much with such slender resources and with so very little adventitious aid as the Society for the Protection of Ancient Buildings.

It was only the other day, so to speak, that a handful of men, whose hearts were in the right place, banded themselves together to raise the voice of warning against a fashion which had become a rage, and which was threatening to make a clean sweep of all that was most venerable, most precious, most unapproachably inimitable in the architectural remains of our country.

Undeterred by the clamour of incompetent impostors, undismayed by the ridicule of people of importance, undiscouraged by the difficulties which must be expected by all gallant crusaders, the little band went forth—a real Salvation Army without drums and without any flourish of trumpets— to save what remained from the devastation that had been going on, not despising the day of small things. They were an audacious band; they proclaimed that the taste and the sentiment of the world had got into an utterly vicious groove— that the taste and the sentiment of the world needed to be corrected, set aright—educated in fact—and that they were going to educate it whether the world liked being educated or not.

Astonishing presumption! "Who are ye?" said the perplexed world,—"who are ye; the apostles of a new toryism, ye that preach the keeping up of the old, which time and tide, the storms and the elements, have pronounced to be moribund? Who are ye that would watch over the homes of the bats and the owls in this our age of advance, with the works of the men of mind rising up to heaven to rebuke you? Ruin-mongers that ye be, prating about the loveliness of mild decay, while we live in the days of carving by machinery, and ashlar smoothed to the likeness of the loveliest stucco by the help of the modern stone plough, and windows that no age ever saw the like of till now, and the smuggest of pulpits and the slipperiest of tiles, and the tallest of walls built of, if not daubed with, the most untempered of mortar? Who are ye? Are ye to be your brothers' keepers?"

Well! all this was very terrible, especially that last thrust! But even that last thrust seemed to read very like a leaf from the book of the first murderer; seemed, too, as if some modern confederates of Cain were afflicted with that same irritable temperament, that same jealousy of being called to account for their misdeeds, which would even go the length of justifying the slaughter of Abel if it should be made to appear that the dead could not be restored to life again.

But the new Reformers, whatever they may have thought, were content to hold their peace. They went peeping and prying about and protesting; they exposed the gross ignorance of an adventurer here; they issued a serious warning to a well-meaning gentleman there; they did as other apostles have done before now—they were instant in season and out of season; they reproved, rebuked, exhorted; and almost before they knew where they were, they discovered that they had many more supporters than at first they had suspected, that the world had been waiting for them this long time back, and that they had started upon their mission not a day too soon.

As soon as people begin to succeed in any mission, they are pretty sure to get into bad odour by the excesses of their more impassioned supporters. Then follow disclaimers, explanations, recriminations, and they are comforted by the reminder that "when fools fall out wise men get their due." When this point has been reached, the other side begins to take heart, and mis-statement is apt to be accepted as the explanation of over-statement, just as now it is beginning to be believed that *Antirestoration* is a full and sufficient summing up of what is meant by the word *Protection*, and that doing nothing is all that this Society aims at.

If there are some crazy fanatics who have injured the cause which they have at heart by advocating in a furious way that all we have to do with an ancient building is to let it alone, and leave it to fall down, rather than do anything to preserve it, I for one hereby declare that I hold such fanatics to be heathen men and heretics of the worst kind. I look upon such people much as I look upon those peculiar people who denounce the whole medical profession as interferers with the laws of Providence, and who forbid the members of their sect from ever setting a broken bone or taking a prescription when sickness or infirmity has attacked them. To talk of letting an ancient building take its chance, and doing nothing to prolong its life, is to my mind to talk pestiferous nonsense with which I have no manner of sympathy. But unhappily there has been another view which has been put forward in a very specious and ingenious and captivating manner by another set of people, and which unhappily has met with immense favour at the hands of the moneyed public, and which seems to me to find its exact parallel in the proposal of a certain unfortunate lady who suffered martyrdom for her faith, or at any rate her profession, some years ago. That poor lady proclaimed to the world that she was so profoundly versed in all the virtues of certain mysterious herbs and salves and potions and mixtures, that she was prepared to guarantee the perfect restoration of youth and loveliness to the most aged and most battered of her sex; in fact, she asserted that she had discovered the grand secret of making them "beautiful for ever." She was, I take it, the high priestess and prophetess of *restoration.*

Now between the criminal and indolent neglect of those who would sit down with folded hands and never stretch out a finger to avert the death of the stricken, and the pretentious puffery of quacks who assure us that they have discovered the secret of rejuvenescence, there is a whole world of difference, and between the stupid do-nothingism of the one and the rash do-everythingism of the other there is—there must be—a middle course. This is what we have to complain of, that when well-meaning people have set themselves to "restore" a church (for I shall keep myself to that branch of the subject for the present), some of us have found the greatest difficulty in learning *what* they were going to restore.

When these good and well-meaning people take it into their heads that an ancient ecclesiastical building is to be replaced by a modern structure in which "all the characteristic features of the original are to be reproduced and for the most part retained," we ask ourselves with wide-open eyes of amazement and perplexity what is going to be reproduced? There is a sumptuous Norman doorway, there are abundant indications of the existences of a Norman church having existed on this spot—there are clear proofs that the Norman pillars have been recklessly cut away here to make room for a splendid thirteenth-century tomb, that the north aisle is an addition raised up at the sacrifice of the original north wall—that a chapel of no great artistic merit was added at another time, that the pitch of the roof was altered when the clerestory was added, that the chancel was rebuilt, flimsily, faultily, fantastically, just before the final rupture with Rome,—and yet that the remains of the superb sedilia which the seventeenth-century mob smashed to pieces were evidently removed from the earlier chancel by the fifteenth-century architects. There are signs, in fact, of the church never having been left undisturbed—that from generation to generation the rude forefathers of the hamlet were always doing something to their church, taking a pride in adding to or altering it, according to their notions. They never thought of *reproducing* anything, but rightly or wrongly they were always aiming at *improving* everything. You are going to restore, are you? *What* are you going to restore? The Norman, the Early English, the Decorated, or the Perpendicular church? What are the characteristic features of the original? What is your notion of the original which you pretend to be about to restore? The problem that presents itself becomes more difficult, more complex, the longer you look at it—the problem, namely, *what* you are going to restore.

If my dear old grandmother should wish to be made "beautiful for ever"—*i.e.* to be restored—what condition of former loveliness shall we call back? There are some who paid homage to her beauty at eighteen, some who loved her at thirty, and some who almost adored her at threescore years and ten. Look at her portraits! Which shall we take? Nay! I love her as she is, say I, with the smile that plays about her venerable lips and the soft light in the gentle eyes. I love every furrow on her broad brow and would not have the thin grey hairs turned to masses of auburn. I would keep her for ever if I might, but I would no more dream of restoring her to what she was before I was born than I would replace her by something that she is not and never was.

Now up and down this land of England there are, say, 5,000 churches that at this moment stand upon the same foundations that they stood upon 500 years ago, some few of them standing in the main as they were left eight centuries ago. If for 5,000 any one should suggest not 5,000, but 10,000, I should find no fault with the correction.

If we could go back in imagination to the condition of these churches as they were left when the Reformation began, it may safely be affirmed that there was not at that time, there never had been, and there is never likely to be again, anything in the world that could at all compare with our English churches. There never has been an area of anything like equal extent so immeasurably rich in works of art such as were then to be found within the four seas. The prodigious and incalculable wealth stored up in the churches of this country in the shape of sculpture, glass, needlework, sepulchral monuments in marble, alabaster, and metal—the jewelled shrines, the precious MSS. and their bindings, the frescoes and carved work, the vestments and exquisite vessels in silver and gold, and all the quaint and dainty and splendid productions of an exuberant artistic appetite and an artistic passion for display which were to be found not only in the great religious houses, but dispersed about more or less in every parish church in England, constituted such an enormous aggregate of precious forms of beauty as fairly baffles the imagination when we attempt to conceive it. There are the lists of the *church goods*— *i.e.* of the contents of churches—by the thousand, not only in the sixteenth century but in the fourteenth: there they are for any one to read; and, considering the smallness of the area and the poverty of the people, I say again that the history of the world has nothing to show which can for one moment be compared with our English churches as they were to be found when the spoilers were let loose upon them.5 Well! We all know that a clean sweep was made of the *contents* of those churches. The locusts devoured all. But the *fabrics* remained— the fabrics have remained down to our own time—they are as it were the glorious framework of the religious life of the past. There is no need for me to dwell upon the claim which these survivals of a frightful conflagration have upon us for safe custody. I presume we all acknowledge that claim, and the only question is how best to exhibit our loyalty. But when we have got so far we are suddenly met by a wholly unexpected and anomalous difficulty before we can make a single step in advance.

Now I am free to confess that hardly a day of my life passes in which I am not oppressed by the conviction that there are few men of my age within the four seas who are as deplorably ignorant of things in general as I feel myself to be;—but there is one branch of ignorance, if I may use the expression, which

I am convinced that the enormous majority of my most gifted acquaintances are sharing with myself—I really do not know to whom these thousands of churches belong.

There was a time when the church belonged to the parish as a sort of corporation, and when by virtue of their proprietary right in their church the parishioners were bound to keep the fabric in tenantable repair. But when that obligation was removed by the abolition of Church rates (so far as I can understand the matter), the church practically ceased to belong to any one. Tell the most devoted church people in my parish that because they are church people therefore they are bound to keep the fabric in repair, and they would to a man become conscientious nonconformists in twenty-four hours. Tell my most conscientious nonconformists that next Monday there is to be a meeting in the vestry and an opportunity of badgering the parson, and not a man of them but would claim his right to be there:—because, under circumstances which are favourable to his own interests and inclinations, every inhabitant of a certain geographical area protests that he is a shareholder in his parish church. It is true that on a memorable occasion I was presented with the key of my church, and was directed to lock myself in and ring the bell, and then was solemnly informed that I had taken possession of my freehold. I daresay it was quite true, only I am quite certain nobody did believe it at the time and nobody does believe it now. From that day to this I never have been able to understand to whom my church does belong.

Now as long as it is only a question of letting things drift the question of ownership never troubles anybody. I am in the habit of telling my people that if the Church of our parish were to be swallowed up by an earthquake some fine morning, there would be only one man who would be a gainer by the catastrophe, and that man would be the rector. For his benefice would at once become a sinecure, and there would be nothing to prevent his removing to the metropolis and living there during some months of the year, and living in the Riviera during the other months, and leaving his people to shift for themselves—nothing to prevent this except those trifling considerations of duty and conscience which of course need not be taken into account. But when it comes to a question of *preventing* the church from tumbling down, or when it comes to a question of pulling it about—when it comes to *restoring* it—

then practically the ownership is surrendered to the parson in the frankest and the freest and the most generous way by the whole body of the parishioners. Then the parson is allowed to be the only responsible owner of the fabric. It is remembered that he rang the bell when he came into his freehold: therefore it must be his; and if he does not take the whole burden of collecting the money and seeing the work through and making himself personally responsible for the cost, in nine cases out of ten it will not be done at all.

Now I am not the man to speak with disrespect of my brethren of the clergy. I do not believe that in any country or in any age there was ever a body of men so heartily and loyally trying to do their duty, and so generously sacrificing themselves to what they believe to be their duty, as the clergy of the Church of England are at this moment. But, whether it is their misfortune or their fault—and we are none of us faultless, not even the parsons—I am bound to express my belief that ninety-nine out of every hundred of the clergy of the Church of England know no more about the technical history of their churches than they know about law—in fact, as a body, the clergy know as little about the history of Church Architecture as lawyers know about Theology, and I could not put the case more strongly than that.

Unhappily, however, the parallel between the amiable weakness of the two professions and their relative attitude towards the two sciences in which each of them delights to dabble may be carried out only too closely. For it is painfully observable in both cases that the members of the two professions are profoundly convinced—the lawyers that a knowledge of theology, the divines that a knowledge of architecture, comes to them severally by a kind of legal or clerical instinct. If a lawyer chooses to plunge into scientific theology, and to write a book on the two Decalogues, or give us his *obiter dicta* on the errors of the Greek Church, though nobody is much the wiser nobody is much the worse, except the man who reads the pamphlet or the volume. But when it has been decided that a church requires a thorough overhauling, then the resigning the absolute control over and disposal of the sacred building to the parson to be dealt with as he in his wisdom or his ignorance may judge to be best becomes a very much more serious matter.

It would be easy to look at that matter from the ludicrous point of view, but it is a great deal too serious for handling as though it were anything to laugh at. Unhappily, we most of us know a great deal too much about it. The parson in some cases jauntily determines to be his own architect, and the village bricklayer highly approves of his decision, and assures him in strict confidence that architects are a pack of thieves, just as, in fact, jockeys are. The builder begins to "clear away," then the parson gets frightened. Then he thinks he'd better have an architect— "only a consulting architect you know!" Then the bricklayer recommends his nephew brought up at the board school who has "done a deal of measurement and that like," and then.... No! no! we really cannot follow it out to the bitter end. But in many cases where the good man, distrusting his own power, does call in the help of one supposed to be an expert, the process and the result are hardly less deplorable. There is nothing to prevent the most ignorant pretender from starting as an architect to-morrow morning; nothing to prevent his touting up and down the country for orders, though he is no more qualified to advise and report upon an ancient building than he is to construct the Channel tunnel. And we all know this very significant fact, that there never was a church that ever was reported upon by one of these solemn and aspiring young gentlemen without antecedents and without any misgivings, which was not at once pronounced to be in a most dangerous condition from weathercock to pavement. The roof is always in a most hopeless condition, the walls are frightfully out of the perpendicular and have been so for many generations, the bells jiggle alarmingly in their frames, the jackdaws have been pecking away at the mortar of the tower, fifty rectors lie buried in the chancel, and a hole was dug for every one of them, and all these holes imperatively demand to be filled up with concrete. But mercifully, most mercifully and providentially, a professional gentleman has been called in at the critical moment, exactly in the very nick of time, and now the dear old church may be saved, saved for our children's children by being promptly restored. Thereupon the worthy parson—he, too, glad of a job—sets to work and the thing is done.

But *what* is done? The men that started this Society, this union for the protection of the noble structures that are a proud inheritance come down to us from our ancestors, they answered with an indignant protest: "An immense and irreparable wrong is done, and the state of things which makes it perfectly easy for a wrong like this to be repeated every week is a shameful national scandal, which we will not cease from lifting up our voices against till some means shall have been devised for preventing the periodical recurrence of these abominable mutilations, these cruel obliterations, these fraudulent substitutions up and down the land of new lamps for old ones."

At starting this was all that our pioneers ventured to proclaim. I have often heard people object, "These gentlemen are so vague, they don't know what they would be at!" Now, I know that with some folk it is quite sufficient to condemn any men or any opinions to pronounce them *vague*. Why! Since the beginning of the world no great forward movement, no great social religious or political reform, has ever achieved its object and gone on its victorious course conquering and to conquer which did not pass through its early stage of vagueness—that stage when the leaders were profoundly conscious of the existence of an evil or an injustice or a falsehood which needed to be swept away, though they did not yet see what the proper manner of setting to work was, or where the broom was to be found to do the sweeping with.

Oh ye merciful heavens! save us from cut-and-dried schemes, at least at starting! All honour to the men, say I, who did not pledge us all to a scheme, to a paper constitution, but who had the courage to say no more than this: "Here in the body politic there is a horrible mischief at work; the symptoms are very bad, very alarming. Do let us see if some remedy cannot be found. Do help us to see our way out of our perplexity."

Eleven years have now gone by since the Society for the Protection of Ancient Buildings was founded, and I venture to think that the time has come when we must pass out of this stage whose characteristic is said to be vagueness of statement and uncertainty in the plan of operations, and when it behoves some one to speak out and propose that we should take a step in advance. I have no right to compromise my betters by pledging them to any crude proposition, or any course which may seem to myself to be the right one. But, as a mere private person, I hereby declare it to be my strong opinion that no time ought to be lost in settling the very important question to whom the churches of England do belong, and who have the right of defacing, degrading, debasing the temples of God in the land, turning them into blotchy caricatures, or into lying mummies smalmed over with tawdry pigments, like the ghastly thing in Mr. Long's picture in the Academy this year, with an effeminate young pretender in the foreground making a languid oration over the disguised remains of the dead.

There are some things (and they are the most precious of all things) which no man has any moral right to treat as his own. They are the things which came to us from an immemorial past, and which belong to our children's children as much as to ourselves. In the county of Norfolk we have one aged oak that has stood where it stands now for at least a thousand years. Under its shadow twenty generations of a noble race have passed their childhood and early youth, left it with a fond regret when the call came to them to engage in the battle of life, and returned at last to find it still there, hale and vigorous as it was centuries before the earliest of their ancestors settled in the land where its mighty roots are anchored. The story of that race is full of romance not untinged by pathos. If that oak were a talking oak, what moving tales it could tell! If 'Arry 'Opkins of 'Ounslow should cast his fishy eyes upon that monster vegetable, his first impulse would be to carve upon its gnarled bark his own hideous name or at least those two unhappy initials which he cannot pronounce. His next would be to suggest that the tree should be trimmed up—restored in fact. I should not like to be the man to make that proposition. And why? Because I think the noble gentleman who calls that oak his heirloom looks upon it as a sacred trust which he holds from his forefathers, and holds for his posterity too—a trust which it would be dishonour to neglect, to mutilate, or to destroy.

But within a pistol-shot of that venerable and magnificent tree stands the little village church. There lie the bones of twenty generations of De Greys; there they were baptized, wedded, buried. There they knelt in worship, lifted up their voices in prayer and praise; from father to son they bowed their heads at the altar, gazed at the effigies of their ancestors—sometimes bitterly lamenting that the times were evil and poverty had come upon them, sometimes silently resolving that they would carve out for themselves a career—sometimes returning to thank God who had enabled them so fully to perform their vow—sometimes glad at the sound of their own marriage bells, sometimes sad when the tolling of those bells announced that another generation had passed away. There stands that little church. The old Norman tower was standing as it stands to-day when, at the beginning of the fourteenth century, the first De Grey came to Merton; and I have not a doubt that if a self-styled professional gentleman, young enough and presumptuous enough and ignorant enough, were to appear upon the scene, he would solemnly and emphatically advise that Merton Church should at the earliest possible moment be restored. The horrible thought is that under quite conceivable circumstances the thing might be done with very little difficulty and before you knew where you were.

Think of the feelings of that old oak then!

I know I shall be told that a tree is one thing and a church is another, that the one you cannot restore but you can restore the other. You can restore neither; you can murder both if you are a heartless assassin. Was it in the 1851 Exhibition that they built up the bark of a giant of the Californian forests and told us it was a restoration of a wonder of the world that had reared up its lofty top to heaven even from the days of the Pharaohs? A restoration! Nay! a colossal fraud. But such a fraud as is perpetrated in our midst every month, and which, when men have committed, they are actually proud of.

I am often asked, When was this or that church built? And my answer is ready at hand. It was not built at all! It grew! For every church in the land that has a real history is a living organism. Do you tell me that yonder doorway is of the twelfth century; that yonder tower may have stood where it does when the Conqueror came to sweep away "pot-bellied Saxondom;" that the chancel was rebuilt in the time of the Edwards—the rood screen crowded into a place never meant for it during the Wars of the Roses, the pulpit supplied by a village carpenter in the sixteenth century, the carvings of the roof destroyed in the seventeenth, the royal arms supplied in the eighteenth, and therefore that nothing but a clean sweep is to be made of it all, as a preliminary to building it all up from the ground in the nineteenth century? Do you call that restoration? You assure me that you will faithfully and religiously copy the old. Why that is exactly what you can't do! You can't copy the marks of the axe on early Norman masonry. You can't copy Roman brickwork; you daren't copy Saxon windows that let the light in through oiled canvas in the days when sacredness, and mystery, and a holy fear were somehow associated with the presence of dimness and darkness and gloom. You can't restore ancient glass: the very secret of its transcendent glories lies in the imperfection of the material employed. Nay, you can't even copy a thirteenth-century moulding or capital: you can't reproduce the carvings you are going to remove—you have no eye for the delicate and simple curves: your chisels are so highly tempered that they are your masters, not your servants: they run away with you when you set to work and insist on turning out sharply cut cusps, all of the same size, all of them smitten with the blight of sameness, all of them straddling, shallow, sprawling, vulgar, meaningless; melancholy witnesses against you that you have lost touch with the living past. You can make the loveliest drawings of all that is left, but the craftsmen are gone. There's where you fail; you say this and that ought to be done, and this or that is what I mean; but when you expect your ideas carried out then you utterly fail.

I know it is often said that the men of bygone times—say of the fifteenth century—were at least as great restorers as we are. If it were true, that would not excuse us. But is it true? Why, so far from it, it is exactly because the architects of the fourteenth and fifteenth centuries did *not* aim at restoring that our modern visionaries so often ask to be allowed to destroy their work and to reproduce what they destroyed. I am no great admirer of those perpendicular gentlemen, with their ugly flattened arches and their huge gaping west windows and their trickery and their pretence and their insincere display, but they did know their own minds. They did retain some architectural traditions, and they had some architectural instincts. But what have we to represent even their instincts? Have our craftsmen anything in the shape of historic enthusiasm? or any sympathy with the religious feeling or ritual of the past? Emphatically, No! Have they the old spirit of humility and reverence, of generous regard for their masters, teachers, and pastors in religion or in art? Have we among us the self-distrust which kept in check the hankering of our forefathers to alter or improve? Or have we only the fidgetty and utterly reckless impatience of belonging to the majority of dismal beings, who never make a great hit and leave no monument behind them except of the things they destroyed?

A few weeks ago I was engaged in examining the muniments of the Diocese of Ely, and I came upon an agreement drawn up in strictly legal form between the Prior of the convent of Ely on the one part and Thomas Peynton, master mason of

Ely, on the other part—the convent agreeing to allow Peynton an annuity for life of twelve marks of lawful money of England—*i.e.* £8 sterling—without board and lodging, and a suit of clothes such as gentlemen wore, he to do such masonry and stone-cutting as the Sacrist of the convent should lay upon him, and further to teach three apprentices, to be nominated, fed, and boarded at the cost of the convent, which in return was to benefit by all the profits of their labour. If the convent should at any time send their master mason to work at any of their outlying possessions, then and only then was the good man to receive an allowance for his maintenance. If his health broke down or he became incapacitated by old age, he was to receive a pension of six marks a year, and his clothes, but nothing more. Who has not stood before some of our cathedrals and found himself asking, "How was this temple piled up to heaven? How could men build it in those rude old times." How? Because in those rude old times, as we are pleased to call them, there were men like simple old Thomas Peynton of Ely, who, having food and raiment, were therewith content; men who lived for the joy and glory of their work and did not regard their art as a means of livelihood, so much as an end to live for; men *who* were so stupid, so far astray, that to sacrifice the joy of living for a mountain of coin seemed to them *propter vitam vivendi perdere causas.*

You will be able to restore the churches which these men built when you can revive among the humblest workmen the spirit which animated the benighted, deluded, Quixotic enthusiasts of the days gone by, and not till then.

Meanwhile, we do know how to build better houses to live in—immeasurably grander hotels, magnificent clubhouses, and sumptuous restaurants. Our bridges and our railway stations, our barracks and our shops, are structures of which we have a right to be proud; but as for our churches, let us be humble, let us forbear from meddling with what we do not understand. Let us pause before we set ourselves to restore, let us be thankful if we are permitted to preserve.

But preserve? How are we going to begin? As a preliminary, as a *sine quâ non,* what is wanted is to stop all unlicensed meddling with all ancient buildings throughout the land. This can only be done by making it quite plain to whom those buildings belong. The ownership of the Houses of God must no longer be left, as it is, an open question. It is absolutely necessary that the present anomalous condition of affairs should be got rid of, and without delay, and I see only one way out of the difficulty. The old churches are a heritage belonging to the nation at large, and now, more than ever before, it is true that the public at large have a claim to be heard before these venerable monuments of past magnificence should be dealt with as if they were the private property of individuals, or of a handful of worthy people inhabiting a minute geographical area. There are cases not a few where the whole population of a parish could be completely accommodated in a single aisle of the village church. In one case that I forbear from naming lest some incompetent and restless aspirant for notoriety should fly upon the spoil and tear it limb from limb—one case of a certain parish where the population is under 200 all told—where there still exists one of the most magnificent churches in England, capable of accommodating at least 1,200 worshippers on the floor, and that church untouched by profane hands for centuries, its very vastness has frightened the most audacious adventurers, and it still stands in its majesty as the wonder and pride of the county in which it is situated.

To restore it according to the notions only too much in vogue would absorb a considerable fortune; to preserve it for future generations, unmutilated, undefaced, and in a condition to defy the elements for centuries, would require a few hundreds; and yet it would probably be easier to find a Crœsus who to gratify his own vanity or whim would be ready to lavish thousands upon that glorious structure and turn it into a gaudy exhibition for nineteenth-century sightseers to come and stare at; easier to find that than to find the hundreds for putting the church into substantial repair. Yet I for one am inclined to think that to do the last is a duty, to do the first would probably end in committing an outrage. When we contemplate such churches as this (and it is by no means a solitary instance), what forces itself upon some of us is that they need first and foremost to be protected before we begin to speak even of repairing them. We talk with pride of our National Church. Is it not time that we should begin to talk of our *National Churches*, and time to ask ourselves whether the ecclesiastical buildings of this country should not be vested in some body of trustees or guardians or commissioners who should be responsible at least for their preservation? Is it not time that we should all be protected from the random experiments of 'prentice hands and the rioting of architectural buffoonery?

All honour to the generous enthusiasm which has urged so many large-hearted men and women in our time to make sacrifices of their substance, not only ungrudgingly but joyfully and thankfully, to make the Houses of God in the land incomparably more splendid and attractive than they were. But even enthusiasm, the purest and noblest and loftiest enthusiasm, if misdirected and uninstructed, has often proved, and will prove again, a very dangerous passion. Before now there have been violent outbreaks of enthusiastic iconoclasm when the frenzy of destroyers has been in the ascendant and when those who would fain preserve the monuments of the past have been persecuted to the death. Is there enthusiasm abroad—enthusiasm to strengthen the things which remain that are ready to die? By all means let it have scope; give it opportunity of action; let it have vent, but beware how you allow it to burst forth into wild excesses; let it be at least kept under control. Build your new churches as sumptuously as you please. Ours is the age of brick and iron, of mechanical contrivances, of comfort and warmth and light. Put all these into your new temples as lavishly as you will, and then peradventure the Church architecture of our own time may take a new departure; but for the old Houses of God in the land, aim at preserving them and do not aim at more!

Let it be enacted that, whosoever he may be, parson or clerk, warden or sidesman, architect or bricklayer, man or woman, who shall be convicted of driving a nail into a rood-screen or removing a sepulchral slab, of digging up the bones of the dead to make a hole for a heating apparatus, bricking up an ancient doorway or hacking out an aperture for a new organ or scraping off the ancient plaster from walls that were plastered five hundred years ago—any one, I say, who shall do any of these acts, even with the very best motives, if he have committed such an offence without the license of a duly constituted authority, shall be adjudged guilty of a misdemeanour and sent to prison without the option of paying a fine. Would you do less in the case of a student at the National Gallery who should presume to restore Gainsborough's "Parish Clerk" or Francia's "Entombment"?

Having made unlicensed meddling with our churches penal, the next thing to be done is to carry out a survey of our churches, and to obtain an exhaustive report upon the condition of all the ancient ecclesiastical buildings in the country which up to this moment have escaped the ravages of the prevailing epidemic. I am afraid the list of such favoured edifices would stagger and horrify us all by its smallness.

The report to be drawn up and published of such a survey as I have ventured to propose would set out to the world an authoritative presentment of the actual condition of each church visited, drawn up by duly qualified and certificated professional men according to instructions laid down for them. The reports should include accurate ground-plans made according to one uniform scale, elaborate copies of mouldings, window-tracery, doorways, capitals, roofs—not merely pretty little sketches suitable for the readers of the *Graphic*, but working drawings, the results of careful measurement; and to this should be added lists of monumental brasses, fonts, remains of mural paintings or ancient glass, a complete register, in fact, of whatever remains the churches contained of ancient work in wood or stone or metal at the time the building was examined and reported on. Of course I shall be met by the objection that the expense of such a survey would be enormous, and that any such scheme is therefore for that one reason impracticable. I am not prepared to go into the estimates. But of this I feel very certain, that, so far from the cost of such a survey and such a publication of reports as those contemplated deserving to be called enormous, it would be much more truly described as insignificant.

The great bulk of the ancient churches which have not been violently tampered with during the last thirty years or so belong to two classes: the very small ones, which have seemed not worth meddling with, and the very large ones which have frightened even the restorers. The cost of drawing up reports upon the small churches would be very trifling and would bring down the average expense considerably, and as to the time required for carrying out such a survey, it need not, I believe, occupy more than three years, though I dare say it might profitably be spread over five. As to any other difficulty standing in the way, it is ridiculous to suggest it. A preliminary survey of all the churches in England was actually begun under the sanction of the Archæological Institute thirty years ago, and a brief report upon the condition of every church in seven counties was published, and may be purchased now for a song. Each church was personally visited by some competent antiquary or architect, and a slight but instructive notice of every edifice was supplied. The survey of the county of Suffolk alone dealt with no less than 541 ecclesiastical buildings of one sort or another. Will it be said that what was so effectively carried out on a small scale by private enterprise thirty years ago could not be done on a large scale now, or that there is less need to do it now than there was in the past generation?

And consider the collateral advantages that would ensue. Consider the immense gain of keeping a band of young architects out of mischief for five years; of inducing them during that time to confine themselves to the severe study of an important branch of their art; of compelling them to become acquainted with the history of its growth and development, and familiarizing them with the minutest detail of Gothic architecture, not in books but *in situ*; and above all of giving them a direct interest in keeping up and preserving some hundreds of ancient buildings which, as things are now, they have actually a pecuniary interest in tempting people to pull down.

But, desirable as it would be—nay, necessary though it be—that some such undertaking as this should be carried through, the other question must come first. Again and again we find ourselves driven back upon that when we attempt to stem the current of vandalism that may happen to be setting in this direction or in that. The ownership of our ecclesiastical edifices must be placed upon a different footing from that which we have acquiesced in too long. Sooner or later this must come; the sooner it comes the better for the interests we have at heart.

*   *   *   *   *

At this point prudence suggests that I should pause. The time has not come for putting forward more than an outline of a proposal which is sure to be denounced as revolutionary. It will be a great point gained if we can find acceptance for the principle advocated. We all do dearly love our own old ways of looking at things; we all do cling tenaciously to the prejudices which we inherited or which were stamped upon our minds in the nursery; we all do honestly detest being worried into changes which interfere with our habits of thought and action and compel us to enter upon some new course. Yet if it be once brought home to us that a great national heritage is being rapidly sacrificed, allowed to perish, or, worse, being wantonly destroyed for lack of that small measure of protection which life and property have a right to expect in every civilized community, I believe that the sense of a common danger will unite men in a generous forgetfulness of their favourite maxims and a shame at their own supineness, and awaken them to see the necessity for concerted action; and then the thing that needs doing will be done.

There was a time in our history when the cry of "the Church in danger" provoked a strange frenzy among the people. The panic did not last very long, and not much came of it. But if another cry should be raised by gentle and simple and men of all creeds and parties, the cry of "the churches in danger!" I do not think little or nothing would come of *that*. That would be not the mere expression of a passing sentiment, but it would be a call to action; and when that cry does come to be raised, the public at large will not be satisfied with anything less than drastic measures, because the nation will have been roused to a consciousness of the value of their heritage; and when a great people begins to assert itself, it is not often that it is content with demanding only what it is morally justified in claiming.

*   *   *   *   *

NOTE.

The following appeared in *The Pall Mall Gazette* of August 15, 1889. If a more dreadful comment upon the above essay can be produced, I have not yet met with it:—

DISESTABLISHMENT BY DEMOLITION.

Mr. Thackeray Turner, the secretary of the Society for the Protection of Ancient Buildings, requests us to publish the following appeal for an ancient church which is in imminent danger of destruction:—

The parish of Sotterley, in the county of Suffolk, lies about five miles from the town of Beccles, and is one of those *close* parishes which they who live in the *opens* are wont to look upon with a suspicion of envy. It is the property of a single owner; not a field or meadow, not a yard of ground by the roadside, not a stake in the hedgerow, not a brick or a gate is to be seen in Sotterley that is not part and parcel of the possessions of the squire and lord of the manor. The estate was for some 400 years held by a family named Playters, which was counted among the great Suffolk houses, and which came to grief at last, partly by taking the wrong side in the troublesome times, and partly by the profuse hospitality which the overgrown size of Sotterley Hall tempted its owners to indulge in. But for four centuries they lived here, and here generation after generation they died and were laid in their graves. In the little church which in life they loved, their bones rest now, and there are their monuments in brass and marble. The walls are studded with their effigies.

Moreover, these Playters—and indeed their predecessors the Sotterleys—spent money and pains upon the sacred building. There to this day stands the fourteenth-century screen in wonderfully good preservation, four at least of the figures in its panels still retaining a great deal of the old brilliancy of colour, though at least 500 years have passed since they were first set up in the position they now occupy. There, too, *in situ* may be seen many of the old oak benches with their handsome "poppy-heads," doubtless carved by Sotterley craftsmen, and carved out of the oaks that were growing in Sotterley wood before the Wars of the Roses had begun. The same roof, which might be easily repaired at an insignificant cost, covers the chancel which covered it before people had dreamed of a Tudor king, the panels but little injured, and of the bosses not one missing.

A man may visit fifty churches in East Anglia, and not meet with one so entirely adapted to the needs of the small population who delude themselves with the preposterous belief that they have a right to worship there.

Moreover, Sotterley Church stands in a churchyard of unusually large dimensions. It must cover at least an acre of ground, and not half of this space shows the smallest sign of interments having been made in it during the present century. But, unhappily, Sotterley Church and churchyard lie in the middle of Sotterley Park—not that it was always so, for the park has come to the church, not the church to the park—and people will insist in going to church, even farmers and farm labourers will, and worshipping the Most High where their forefathers worshipped before them. The Hall of the Playters was pulled down during the last century, and the new hall—an ugly white-brick mansion of no pretension—was set up much nearer to the ancient church; and when Sotterley people died nothing could prevent their relatives from carrying their dead to the old graveyard and laying them where they themselves hoped to lie some day. But was not this a little too bad, to have a funeral procession of tearful clodhoppers passing through your park gates and under your very windows, asking no leave, but taking it in quite a brutal fashion?

Therefore, about ten years ago, a vestry meeting, or something of the sort, was held in Sotterley. The landlord's pleasure was signified, certain formalities were gone through, the tenantry, small and great, were told that it was desirable that Sotterley churchyard should be closed, and, the legal document being duly drawn up, an order was obtained from the Privy Council, and the churchyard was closed accordingly. Outside the park gates, in a place where four ways meet, a square patch of ground, scrubby and soppy, has been fenced off by a mean and ill-kept hedge, and in the middle of it stares rather than stands, a forbidding protuberance, an octagonal construction of cheap Sotterley bricks, covered with cheap Sotterley tiles, looking like a ginger beer stall in a cricket ground where there is no play going on. This thing is called a chapel, I believe, and here the Sotterley people must needs bring their dead. Will they all be brought here? High and low—rich and poor one with another? Well, to get rid of the funerals passing through the park was one point scored; but it was but a beginning. On Easter Monday last a meeting of the parish in vestry assembled was held as usual in Sotterley church. I am told that the parishioners, knowing what was coming, very discreetly kept away, all except the unhappy parson, who was bound to be there, the landlord and one, two, or three others, who, it is suspected, were told to be there. Forthwith a resolution drawn up beforehand was proposed, seconded, and carried unanimously—for the parson had nothing to do but to "put it to the meeting"—to the effect that it was desirable to pull down or shut up the church of Sotterley, and build another somewhere else. I am told that this resolution has been actually forwarded to the Bishop of Norwich and that a faculty has been actually applied for to close or destroy a church which has been standing in its present site for the best part of a thousand years, and that it only remains for the Bishop to give his assent to this iniquitous proposition, and one more of those monstrous outrages will have become an accomplished fact which we English submit to with just a little snarling after they have been committed, and which we allow to be perpetrated under our eyes without ever lifting a finger to prevent. Whether the Bishop of Norwich is the man to connive at so shameful a job as this, and to give his episcopal sanction to the proposed desecration, is a question that is a humiliating one to ask, for is it less than infamous that such things are so possible that we begin to inquire about their probability?

V.
CATHEDRAL SPACE FOR NEGLECTED RECORDS.

THE most delightful place of resort on the face of the globe is to be found within a bow-shot of Temple Bar. Not on the south side of Fleet Street, whatever enthusiastic gentlemen of the law may say, nor on the west, nor on the east, for there too there is little to attract us except in the shop windows, and there is noise and turmoil and the roar of a restless multitude bewildering and disturbing us whether we move or halt on our way. No! my happy valley lies to the north of the great thoroughfare; its courts and halls and corridors, its restful solitudes, its mines of gold that are waiting to be worked, its storehouses of precious things that are practically inexhaustible, all are to be found in a favoured region that lies between Chancery and Fetter Lanes.

"Record Office, Fetter Lane!" I said to the driver of a Hansom some months ago. "Do you mean *Chancery* Lane, sir?" asked the voice through the hole over my head. "No, I mean Fetter Lane." The man actually did not know the situation of the earthly Paradise.

Pone me pigris ubi nulla vicisArbor æstiva recreatur aura,

I murmured to myself—I could not waste my Horace upon Cabby.

I am in the habit of assuring my lowly congregation upon Sundays that for all their talk about heaven they would find themselves very much out of place there without some previous preparation for that desirable abode. The same warning is equally true when applied to other blissful resting-places besides the celestial mansions. You must have a taste for them; you must have qualified yourself to enjoy them and to mix with the company you find there. Surely Valhalla could only have suited the few. But this place of resort of which I am thinking is a pleasure-house whose resources are actually limitless, however well you may have learnt to use your opportunities. "Life piled on life were all too little" to get even so much knowledge of this prodigious and enormous accumulation of treasures as to be able to answer with certainty what may be found there and what not. For eight-and-forty years there has appeared annually a *Report of the Deputy Keeper of the Public Records*, presenting us with an elaborate summary of work carried on by the functionaries employed in examining our national archives; and so far are we from getting to the end of the work of men cataloguing and calendaring that it may reasonably be estimated another fifty years will be required to complete this vast preliminary labour; and when that time comes it will be necessary to begin again at summarizing and supplying indices to the reports issued. What next will follow it is difficult to conjecture or imagine.

The forty-eighth Report, issued in 1887, happens to be lying at my elbow as I write, and there, ready for consultation, I find a brief calendar of the Patent Rolls of the seventh year of Edward the First, drawn up by one of the many accomplished archivists of the Office. It fills 216 closely printed pages. It summarizes at least 3,000 documents, some of them of considerable length; they all belong to a single class, and they are all concerned with the life of our forefathers—yours and mine, my estimable reader—during the single year ending the 20th of November, 1279. Six centuries ago. Think of that! Yet this collection is but one among thousands. The third Report, issued in 1842, first drew attention to the existence of a huge mass of ancient letters of the reigns of King John, Henry the Third, and Edward the First, the most modern of them, observe, coming down no nearer to our own time than the year 1307 A.D. "This important mass," we are told, "appears to contain 1,942 bundles, each containing on the average about 200 documents, or about 388,400 on the whole." Scared by such figures as these, the imagination, a trifle jaded, refuses to dwell upon 913 Papal Bulls of various dates, or to take the trouble to speculate upon the probable bulk of seven or eight thousand documents which reveal unknown secrets about the ancient forests and their boundaries. But we are fairly aghast at the news that there are hundreds of rolls averaging 200 feet in length, and at least one extending to the enormous dimensions of 800 feet, written within and without with lamentation and mourning and woe. There could be no eating such a roll as that!

The documents deposited in the Record Office, and which, as we have seen, are likely to have taken a hundred years to catalogue before they become readily accessible to students and explorers, count by millions. They are of all sorts, conditions, and classes, but they may be roughly described as concerned with the civil and political history of the nation; that is, they deal with the development of our institutions, with the government of our sovereigns through their ministers, with the changes in our laws and their administration, with the complex questions of the tenure of land and the changes in its ownership, with the rise and growth of our commerce, with our wars by land and by sea, with a hundred other matters which never can cease to have a profound and undying interest for the citizens of a great empire. Let us, for convenience' sake, call the Record Office the storehouse of authorities on England's *constitutional* history.

This vast *tabularium*, as the Romans called their Public Record Office, is situated, as I have said, within a bow-shot of Temple Bar, and to the northeast of that vanished structure. About double the same distance on the south-west there exists another huge depository of records, which may be said to be a great storehouse of authorities concerned with our *family* history. The wills which are stored in Somerset House, though beginning at a date centuries later than the early records in Fetter Lane, go back quite far enough to make the reading of the great mass of them not always easy for the uninitiated. They, too, probably count by millions, and I have known one gentleman who estimated the number which he himself had looked at and examined with more or less attention at not less than a hundred thousand. This collection is more easily accessible to students than the other, inasmuch as here we are dealing with a single class of documents, which present no difficulties of arrangement, and which have been carefully preserved and habitually consulted for generations, and are as a rule bound up in big volumes of transcripts, or offices copies, made for the most part within a short time of the original wills having been proved before the accredited officials. So far as they go the wills in Somerset House contain to a very great extent the *genealogical* history of England. It is necessary to guard this statement by qualifying words, for the wills in Somerset House are the wills of men and women who died in the southern province only.

If we lengthen our radius, keeping to Temple Bar as our centre and sweeping a circle say of five miles in diameter, we shall include within this circumference a vast collection of records of a very miscellaneous character. There are the muniments of the City of London; there is an unknown mass of curious "evidences" in the secret chambers of the London companies;

there are the mysterious and probably very large stores of recondite lore hidden away somewhere in the great Inns of Court, and perhaps in forgotten garrets of some of the minor dependencies of those august institutions. There are the sessional records of the county of Middlesex, which a very moderate estimate has assured us contain more than half a million documents; and, in addition to all these, there are probably many other important collections subsidiary to these larger ones, the very existence of which is unknown and unsuspected except by some few reticent creatures, who with the grip of the miser cling secretively to the hoarded treasures that they cannot spend and will not let any one else look at. It must be evident to any one who reflects upon the measureless bulk—the mere bulk—of these various assemblages of ancient documents to be found within the metropolitan area alone, that any heroic policy which should contemplate gathering them all under a single roof, and unifying them in a centralized national *tabularium*, is inpracticable. A Public Record Office which should not only be a monster warehouse for the safe custody of our ancient muniments, but should be a library of reference open to all duly qualified persons desirous of pursuing historical research among our unprinted sources, would be a building that would more than fill Trafalgar Square. Obviously such a collection, to be practically accessible, would require to be methodized, arranged, catalogued, and to some extent indexed. An army of trained officials would be needed to deal with the materials under their hands. It would take a lifetime to set the house in order. The very geography of such a world would require a guide-book as perplexing as a Bradshaw.

The magnificent collection now at the Record Office is, as has been seen, only in course of being examined and calendared. Even after fifty years of unremitting labour bestowed upon it we have a very imperfect knowledge of what it contains; and this, be it remembered, though no department of the public service can compare with this in the ability, industry, enthusiasm, and profound learning which have been for generations the characteristic of the officials, one and all, high and low. From the days of that cross-grained, combative, and overwhelmingly learned miracle of erudition William Prynne down to our own day there has been a kind of apostolical succession among the keepers of the national archives and their coadjutors. The Record Office almost deserves to have a dictionary of biography of its own. To widen the field of labour here would be to destroy all hope of its ever being brought into order. Centralization of our muniments has well-nigh reached its utmost limits in the unwieldy proportions of the collection now under the charge of the Deputy Keeper. To extend those limits and to bring together additional millions of MSS. from distant depositories would be to convert the great *tabulariumn* into a colossal *cæmeterium*, in which they would be not so much preserved as buried for all time.

Let it be conceded, then, that, as far as the Record Office is concerned, it will be best to leave well alone. The custodians of our archives in Fetter Lane have quite enough to occupy their time for many a long day. They are not the men to need urging or to embarrass by loading them with new accessions of work which they can never hope to get through. On the other hand, the muniments of such bodies as the great Inns, the chartered companies, or the Corporation of London can hardly—at any rate hardly *yet*—be looked upon and dealt with as public property. These corporations very naturally cling to their own possessions; they are jealous of throwing open their muniments to be scrutinized and peeped into by prying eyes by no means always looking with a kindly or benevolent gaze. Why should the benchers of the Middle Temple, for instance, lay out their early charters to be copied by every chance grievance-monger, to be printed with appropriate comments in the columns of the *Wapping Watchman*, and enriched by learned notes and illustrations full of love and sweetness? Why should the ancient Guild of the Girdlers court publicity when there is a host of Grub Street ragamuffins only too glad to make merchandise of their "Curious Revelations" and to ferret out inconvenient scraps of information to be used for the destruction of the things that are? "Confound that shabby old Dryasdust!" we might hear the warden growl out to his brethren of the craft. "If the fellow goes on like that we shall have to ask him to dinner, give him a bad one, and protest we could not afford a better in the lamentable condition of our finances." No! Diligent explorers and omnivorous antiquaries like my friend Mr. Cadaverous must be patient and submissive. "The rights of property, sir—the rights of property must be respected. Make your approaches in a spirit of courtesy and with becoming respect for the august body to which we belong, and you may find us gracious and condescending; but come to us as a footpad grabbing at our fobs, and you may find the consequences disastrous. We have been known to give pence to beggars, but to submit to be plundered—never!"

There is, however, one class of documents to be found within the area that I have been dealing with which may fairly be regarded as public property in a different sense from that in which the civic and corporate muniments can be considered such. I refer to the registers and churchwardens' books, which constitute an important collection of records from which a great deal of our parochial and family history may be gleaned. I know how contemptuously some good folks affect to treat pedigree-hunting and genealogy. I know how much ridicule has been heaped upon the pompous pettiness of beadles and vestrymen. Mr. Bumble in a Punch and Judy show or in a Christmas pantomime is always greeted with a welcome of convulsive merriment. And yet somehow we all do feel some sly hankering to know how they managed it in the parochial councils, say, two or three hundred years ago; and few men are so indifferent as some dull men pretend to be about the mere bare births, deaths, and marriages of their forefathers. It may be very profitless, very silly, but so is playing at chess, and smoking, and many another harmless diversion. And is that all?

I am not going to enter into the question of what larger and wider fields of enquiry the humbler by-paths of research may help us to pass through without going helplessly astray; but this is certain, that there never has been a civilized nation since nations grew into organized life—never has been, never will be—in which something like a passion for finding out the smaller secrets of the past has not been strong, and in some minds absorbing. Be that as it may, there are, it may be estimated, some hundreds of volumes scattered about in all sorts of odd places, in the custody of all sorts of odd people, within the metropolitan area which contain the entries of the three most important events in the lives of millions of people who have been born, wedded, and died within five miles of Temple Bar during the last three centuries and a half. These volumes are being consulted every week. Copies of the entries made in them are produced as evidence in courts of justice every month, and vast sums of money change hands every year on the testimony which those books afford, and almost upon that alone. On that testimony again and again the title to large estates, the right to seats in the House of Lords, the legitimacy of son or daughter, has depended. Fiction and fact have vied with each other in emphasizing the romantic incidents that our parish registers have chronicled or concealed. All the existing parish registers within the metropolitan area, from the year 1538 (when parish registers first began to be kept in England) to the beginning of the present century, and all the churchwardens' books besides, might easily be kept in a single room of Somerset House, and be easily supplied with perfect personal indices in five years.

*   *   *   *   *

One more class of ancient records remains to be dealt with before we leave London and its purlieus. Nothing has yet been said of that immense mass of precious muniments which constitute the apparatus from which the *ecclesiastical* history of England may be compiled; that is, the history of the part which the Church has played in the political, religious, and, I may add, the moral and intellectual training and education of the nation.

There are within little more than a mile of our old friend Temple Bar three great depositories of ecclesiastical records of inestimable value and of unknown richness—one at the Archiepiscopal Palace of Lambeth, one at St. Paul's, one in the precincts of Westminster Abbey. (1) The collection of MSS. at Lambeth was very ably catalogued nearly eighty years ago, and is readily accessible to all who are desirous and competent to make an intelligent use of the treasures it contains. (2) The archives of St. Paul's comprehend not only the muniments of the great Metropolitan Chapter, but those also of the bishopric of London. The Chapter records have been examined and reported upon by the present Deputy Keeper in the *Ninth Report of the Historic MSS. Commission.* Of course Mr. Lyte has done his work in a masterly way, and to the wonder and despair of smaller men who have tried their 'prentice hands at such employment; but he warns us that "the greater part of the collection *has never yet been examined for literary or historical purposes*;" and so far from this important assemblage of original documents being accessible to research, Mr. Lyte, when he began his examination, found it stowed away in boxes "in an octagonal chamber above the Dean's vestry," and one box full of ancient documents had been discovered by the Bishop of Oxford "in a loft over the Chapter House." The extent, interest, and importance of the capitular records to historical students is in the present condition of our knowledge quite incalculable.

But the archives of the *diocese* of London are also said to be kept in St. Paul's. Thirty years ago, when I was very young at this kind of work, I obtained permission to make a search among the muniments of the Bishop of London for certain small fragments of information which, in the glorious hopefulness of youth, I was bent on discovering. During three short December days I was privileged to climb to a certain chamber in a certain tower of St. Paul's, and there to immure myself for five or six hours at a time. There is a region where beings who succeed in retaining their personality must needs be the sport of the vortices that whirl and eddy through the "vast inform," where "Chaos umpire sits" and "next him high arbiter Chance governs all." But in such a region none may hope to find anything that he can carry away. I emerged from that three-days' audacious voyage of discovery with my intellect only a little disordered and my constitution only a trifle shattered, and I survive to speak of that bewildering and horrible experience as men speak of their confused recollection of an escape from drowning. From that day to this I have never met with a human being who had ever been bold enough to search among the archives of the bishopric of London or who could tell me anything about them, good or bad.

(3) Somewhere—somewhere—within the precincts of the great Abbey of Westminster there are said to be imprisoned in grim and forbidding seclusion unknown multitudes of witnesses, voiceless, tongueless, forgotten, whose testimony, if it could be extorted, would strangely and powerfully affect our views upon hundreds of incidents and movements, hundreds of crimes and errors and sacrifices and grand endeavours that now are very imperfectly understood, often wholly misrepresented, and some of them passed out of remembrance. Let us take an example.

We have all of us heard of the *Star Chamber*. Pray may I ask my accomplished readers if they know anything about the Stars? Nay! Be not rash with thy lips. The name Star Chamber has not the remotest connection with astronomy. The name carries us back to a time when the children of Israel were swarming in England and when they were the great bankers or money-lenders—almost the only bankers and money-lenders—within the four seas. Impecunious scoundrels up and down the land mortgaged their lands or pawned their valuables, and the Jews advanced them money upon their securities. The promises to pay, the agreements to surrender property on non-payment, the bonds, the bills, the orders of court, and the documentary evidence bearing upon all these transactions between the creditors and the debtors, the borrowers and the lenders, were drawn up in the Hebrew language, and the records of these multifarious transactions between the Jews and the Christians, dating back to an unknown antiquity (possibly to a time very little after the Conquest) and *ending* about the year 1290, when all Jews were banished from England with unspeakable acts of cruelty and wrong—these records, I say, are to be found in the archives of Westminster Abbey. These Hebrew records are believed to count by thousands, and are known by the name of *stars* among the few who even know that there are such things in existence. As to the exact meaning or derivation of the word, I dare not venture upon an explanation of it; nor as to the correct spelling of it am I qualified to express an opinion. It is sufficient for me that the court in which these suits between the Jews and their victims, or their defrauders, were tried and decided was in ancient times called the *Star* Chamber, because the records of the proceedings which were there adjudicated upon were popularly known as *stars*. Perhaps not six men in Britain have ever looked *intelligently* at this mass of Hebrew MSS. I believe only one man living—Mr. Davies—has devoted any time to the study of them. And yet with this immense and unique apparatus absolutely untouched, with this virgin soil that has been neglected and unknown for six centuries, literary empirics have more than once set themselves to write the history of the Jews to the Middle Ages, "resorting to their imagination for their facts" when the facts were there at their elbows if they had only known it. The history of the Jews in England down to the time of their expulsion by Edward the First remains to be written, because the materials for that history have remained to the present hour unread.

Take another instance. There have been many very interesting books printed about Westminster Abbey; about the sovereigns that were crowned there, about sovereigns that were buried there, about dramatic incidents that occurred within the glorious church, about its architecture, about its school, about its single bishop and its many illustrious deans. The magnificent and venerable institution is so spangled with golden memories that the dryest handbook must needs prove attractive to the dullest of readers. The whole place in its every stone and nook and corner is wrapped in an atmosphere of romance and wonder and mystery; but anything that deserves to be called by so grand a name as a History of Westminster Abbey, or anything approaching to it, can no more be said to exist than can the History of Carthage or Damascus. There may be, there is, some excuse for our ignorance in the one case, but in the other case there is none. There, within the very walls where the history was a-making through the ages, in the very handwriting of the men whose lives were passed within the precincts and who were actors in the drama of which they left their fragments of notes or scraps of illustrations or briefest mementoes, there, huddled together in bunks and trunks and sacks and boxes—no one can tell you exactly where—there is such a wealth of materials that when it comes to be methodized and utilized, digested and studied, as it *must* be some day, the result will inevitably be to make the men of the future look with larger, other eyes than ours upon the action of those forces and the character of those movements, and the statesmanship of those leaders and commanders of the people which have worked together in the evolution of a great nation from its inchoate condition of a mere gathering of peoples. Nevertheless, for any facilities that exist for studying the records of Westminster Abbey they might almost as well be kept in glass cases in the moon as be where they are. Am I, then, going to propose...? My good sir, I am going to propose nothing, nothing at any rate with regard to the London records, lay or clerical. Only this I venture to remark, that before we have taken stock of our metropolitan muniments and got them into order, before we have provided suitable receptacles for them and put them under the charge of qualified custodians, we shall be wiser if we learn a little modesty in talking about other people and other places, and what they ought to do and what ought to be done for them.

*   *   *   *   *

Once upon a time there was a grizzly monster who sat himself down in the neighbourhood of the ancient city of Thebes. He was a ravenous monster with an insatiable appetite, and he demanded for his meals large supplies of Theban youths and maidens. The monster conducted himself in a very exacting and insolent manner, and somehow he contrived to make the unhappy Thebans acquiesce in his bold assumption that the gods had created Thebes and all that belonged to it for no other purpose under heaven than for the support and glorification of his own unwieldy self, growing daily more corpulent, voracious, and overbearing. At last one fine day the monster in a sportive humour asked the Thebans a riddle, and a sagacious gentleman guessed the riddle. The answer was "Man." It was a very curious conundrum, and when the answer came it brought with it an important and startling suggestion. "Ye burghers of Thebes," one cried, "look to it! Man was *not* created for the monster! That be far from us! Monsters peradventure there must be—some beneficent, some malign, some to be proud of, some to loathe. But be they what they may, let it be ours to proclaim, Not man for the monsters, but monsters for the behoof of man!" That wholly novel and unexpected resolution, having been carried unanimously and by acclamation, wrought quite a revolution among the Theban folk. I am sorry to say its effect upon the voracious creature aforesaid was disastrous. They say he did not wait to perish of famine, but died violently of a ruptured heart.

There is among us a school of pundits, who live and always have lived within the sound of Bow Bells, whose Dagon and Baal and Moloch and Juggernaut combined is London, whose Gospel is "Blessed are they whom the great city vouchsafes to devour." Outside the five-miles circle, or the ten-miles circle, these men think there are indeed certain insignificant atoms, minute, nebulous, meteoric, held in solution in that impalpable medium which for convenience has been called by idealists the realm of England, but that these purposeless particles have no sort of cohesion, and their continuance even as atoms can only be assured in so far as they are destined to become integral portions of that vast pleroma the all-embracing and all-devouring London. No! Let it be proclaimed upon the housetops, let the protest go forth and awake the echoes, "England does not exist for London, but London for England!" Let men ponder that profound and pregnant utterance of the greatest of our historians—"From the beginning of its political importance London acts constantly as the pulse, sometimes as the brain, *never perhaps in its whole history as the heart of England.*" Is that so? Then let us beware how we give our monster more than its due and more than it can manage, lest it develop into a hydrocephalous monster with a pulse that beats but feebly by reason of its life's blood being scantily supplied.

Indeed, it is easy to exaggerate the value and importance even of the metropolitan archives. To begin with, the records of the City of London will be found of little or no use for investigating the history of English agriculture. What will they teach us about the complex questions of land tenure, the life of the peasantry, the relations between the lords and the tenants of the soil, about the condition of the people, high and low, about those local courts and franchises and customs, and disciplinary and formative machinery, which "through oppression prepared the way for order and by routine educated men for the dominion of law"? You must go a long way out of London to get anything like a grasp of the constitution of a county palatine, and to understand the working, if I may use the expression, of such forms of local government as were once active in the manor, the honour, or the hundred. You must study such matters not only in the rolls and charters that survive, but you must study them too in the geographical areas with which they are concerned. What! gather together all the parish registers, and all the wills and all the sessional papers within the four seas and toss them all together into a vast heap "somewhere" in London! What for? That a score or two of cockney dryasdusts may have the opportunity of getting at them by a short ride outside a "penny bus"? Why, you might just as well propose that all the parish churches should be carted away bodily and set up "somewhere" in battle array as a kind of ecclesiastical wall round the metropolis, in order to give adequate facilities of study to the Institute of British Architects in Conduit Street.

The fact is that within the last few years more has been done in the way of arranging, cataloguing, and providing for the safe custody of ancient documents in the provinces than has been even attempted (outside the Record Office) by London and the Londoners. We poor creatures in the wilds, *we* don't go whining for subsidies from the Government, *we* don't clamour for grants from the national exchequer; and there are some of us that can give a very much better account of our muniments than you Londoners can give of yours. Thirty years ago the corporation of Norwich had a catalogue of its records drawn up by a local antiquary, which for convenience of reference and the intimate and wide knowledge it displays could bear comparison with any similar undertaking then existing in the country. The records of the borough of Ipswich, says Mr. J. Cordy Jeaffreson, "are at present so perfectly arranged that with the help of the new catalogue and index ... the custodian can produce without difficulty any charter, roll, or paper account that it may be needful to examine." The records of the corporation of Leicester, says the same learned antiquary, "will endure comparison with the muniments of any provincial borough in Great Britain." The magnificent enthusiasm of two citizens of that same borough has brought this immense assemblage of MSS. into a condition which may well arouse envy and ought to stimulate rivalry; while the example set by the mayor and corporation in making their treasures accessible to all comers proves that enthusiasm is contagious.

These instances are taken at random; there is no need to multiply them. It is well known to experts, and to some who are much less than experts, that the condition of our corporation records throughout the land is very far more satisfactory than was suspected a few years ago, and that every year more and more attention is being bestowed upon them, more vigilance displayed in their preservation, and more zeal and earnestness exhibited in the patient study of their contents. Every year the number of intelligent explorers of our municipal and other local archives is steadily increasing, which means that every year the study of our history is being more laboriously pursued by specialists. For the rest, the whole field is felt to be too vast to travel through in the present state of our knowledge. But just as great laws and great generalizations in physical science have been made, and could only have been made, by the devotion of students concentrating their attention upon a single branch of physiology, chemistry, or astronomy, and registering the conclusions—that is, the certainties— which their several researches have arrived at, so must it be with history; there, too, research must be carried on by men who will be content to labour in a limited area and to deal with problems which cease to be insignificant when their bearing upon larger questions is recognized and the results of one man's toil are affiliated to those of another's.

But if this be so, if indeed the history of England of the future will be the outcome of what may be called the experimental and departmental method of research, it is obvious that the examination of the enormous body of evidence now at our command must be carried on by *local inquiries*. Only so can slight hints and faint clues be apprehended, the local customs and dialects understood, and the very names of places and persons detected in their various disguises. But what we have found ourselves led to suspect when we were dealing with the various collections of records now dispersed in the great hiding-places of London—namely, that sooner or later we shall have to group those records in departmental archives—this we are irresistibly compelled to believe we shall sooner or later have to do with the large masses of historic MSS. which are scattered broadcast over the island from Land's End to John o' Groat's House.

In the smaller world of London—yes, Mr. Gigadibs, the *smaller* world—observe, it is a concession to your stubborn prejudices to call it a world at all, but if a world I protest that the qualifying epithet must be resorted to—in the smaller world of London we have seen that the existing collections of records may be roughly associated in certain groups or classes according as they are regarded as belonging to the evidences bearing upon (1) the history of the monarchy and the development of the constitution; (2) the history of English law and all that concerns such matters as procedure, judicature, and the like; (3) the history of the City of London—of its great guilds, its customs, privileges, and commerce; (4) personal and family history, and (5) lastly, ecclesiastical history, including in that the history of the religious houses. In the wider area we should have to make a similar classification, but in doing so we should have to add one class of documents very inadequately represented in the London collections; I mean those which supply an apparatus for studying the history of the land.

And here we are face to face with a serious difficulty. The evidences, which until the present century were so intimately associated with a landed estate that they passed with the estate as an almost necessary proof that possession had been conveyed, had in the lapse of ages grown in many instances to an aggregate of documents whose bulk was prodigious and its mere stowage embarrassing. Where the capital mansion of an extensive property was proportionate to the acreage it was easy to set apart one room as a muniment-room, in which thousands of charters, court rolls, bailiffs' accounts, and other records were deposited and sometimes arranged with great care and precision; but where a great estate was broken up, or there was no longer any important residence upon it, the evidences often found their way into very strange depositories. The family solicitor had to find a home for them, and to do so was often extremely inconvenient; or the capital mansion became a farm-house, and the evidences were packed in boxes and sent up to the garrets under the roof, in some cases were bundled into the hayloft. By the legislation which simplified the conveyance of land and rendered it no longer necessary to go back to the beginning of time in order to prove a title, the ancient "evidences" became at once valueless for all practical purposes. They became not only useless but odious lumber, and a process of quietly getting rid of them set in and has been steadily carried on to the present moment. The rolls of manor courts and courts leet, which give an insight into the daily life of our forefathers, and which may still be met with in large numbers, dating back to the days of Henry the Third, were destroyed by tens of thousands. Documents which could have thrown light upon some of the most interesting problems which are now being worked at by the profoundest jurists and the most acute students of constitutional history have perished in unknown multitudes. Others which contained invaluable illustrations of local customs—of tyrannous overstraining of feudal authority on the one hand or of crafty evasions of feudal services on the other, of the rapacity of lords and stewards of manors here and of successful appropriations of strips of land or rights of commonage or pasture there—vanished from the face of the earth, none would tell how. The extent to which this destruction of ancient muniments has been carried on cannot yet be even approximately estimated. Nevertheless much remains. The interest which such writers as Mr. Seebohm, Mr. Maitland, Mr. Thorold Rogers, and others have aroused in the many important inquiries which they have severally pursued is increasing day by day, and there can be no doubt that a desire to become better acquainted with the contents of those documents which still survive and may still be rescued and preserved is spreading rapidly and widely. But "where are they to be kept when we have got them?" is the question that presses. It is more than can be expected of the civic authorities that they should charge the rates of the town with providing house room for collections of MSS. which are but remotely concerned with the history of the boroughs themselves. The local museums as a rule are overcrowded and can barely keep their heads above water. The boxes and bundles of rolls and parchments in the lawyers' offices are provokingly in the way; the country houses are changing hands week by week, and Philistines prefer dressing-rooms to muniment rooms. Will no one suggest a way out of our difficulties?

*   *   *   *   *

I have passed very lightly over the condition of affairs at Westminster Abbey and St. Paul's, and that for more reasons than one, the chief reason, but by no means the only one, being that I know nothing about the Abbey muniments or of those of the bishopric of London, and nobody seems able to tell me anything. I have not even alluded to the archdeaconries of the diocese of London.

Those lofty souls whose habit it is to dogmatize most airily when they declaim most ignorantly, are never more jocose than when they take a turn at the archdeacons and their visitations. Well, it is very funny to think of there being any grotesque survivals of such an institution as an archdeacon's court still existing among us. What a droll prelate Bishop Remigius must have been that he actually divided his overgrown and unwieldy diocese of Lincoln into seven archdeaconries about twelve years after the Conquest! How very odd that the successors of those seven functionaries have been going on merrily archdeaconizing down to the present day! How did they amuse themselves all this long time? How did they keep up their little game? "Exercising archidiaconal functions, of course." And of course we are expected to receive that novel explanation with shouts of laughter. Well, but wouldn't you like to know how they really *did* employ themselves? Suppose you were by chance to hear that the action of the archdeacons' courts had *something* to do with the emigration of the Pilgrim Fathers and many hundreds of their friends to New England, say, in the seventeenth century; something perhaps to do with the death of Arch-bishop Laud and the twenty years' imprisonment of Bishop Wren. Wouldn't you like to know something about it all? What have become of the records of the archdeaconries? I know where a few of them are: but where the great mass of them are to be found I know not, and it would take a great deal of trouble to discover. Those that I know of are in closets in lawyers' offices. A blessing on those lawyers, say I, for they have at any rate preserved some fragments of ancient evidences which but for them would have gone to make *glue* long ago. But if you want to find out what the ecclesiastical discipline exercised by the archdeacons upon gentle and simple in the old days was like, you will have to fish up the records of the archdeacons' courts out of their hiding-places, and you will find them to contain some very, very funny items of information, almost as droll as the buffoonery of those lofty souls.

If we are ever to arrive at clearer and truer views of the history of the slow growth of certain moral, religious, and even political convictions among the great body of the people—by the help of, or in despite of, the inquisitorial, coercive, and repressive machinery of the local ecclesiastical courts, which for centuries were exercising a real and terrible power within a ride of every man's door through the length and breadth of the land—we certainly must not neglect that large body of evidence which is to be found in the records of the archdeacons' courts. But it is obvious that such records must be unified, must be made accessible to students, which means, in other words, that they must be collected into diocesan or provincial archives.

So with the parochial registers, churchwardens' books, the wills and other MSS. which are more or less concerned with the private and family life of our ancestors. We have a right to know what our fathers thought and believed, and how they got to break away from this or that superstition, arrived at this or that new truth, were delivered from this or that thraldom, rebelled against this or that wrong, suffered for their errors as if they were crimes, learnt to reverence even doubt when it dawned upon them that doubters could be earnest, noble, and loving, learnt to see that Christian charity could be tolerant even of mistakes; how their horizon widened as their vision became stronger; how as knowledge grew from more to more the old bonds and shackles that cramped the spirit of man became more and more strained even to bursting; how the old fetters bit into the flesh of some, the old chains wore out the hearts and brains of others; how they spoke to their children in their last hours; what messages they sent to friends and kindred when the end was drawing very near; what their hope and trust was as they *looked beyond* the veil. Yes, we have a right to know these things if they are to be known. You may sneer at the follies of pedigree hunters if you will, and deride the harmless madness of genealogists; but I do not envy the man who would not give two straws to find out whether his grandfather's grandfather was a hero or a blackleg, whether he lived the life of a successful pickpocket, or died the death of a martyr for his honest convictions. And if any one is so little acquainted with the curiosities of parish registers, or the contents of parish chests, or the strange secrets often revealed or alluded to in the wills of provincial probate courts, as to suppose that these "rags of time" are wholly wanting in any elements of pathos and romance, he certainly has a great deal to learn, and he knows very little indeed about the contents of documents which he so tranquilly assumes to be "barren all."

From what has been said thus far I hope it will be clear that I am as little inclined to advocate the removal of the municipal records from their proper homes, the muniment rooms of the provincial boroughs, as I am to propose that the archives of London should be transferred from the Guildhall to any other repository. What is wanted is not centralization but classification. Already it has been found advisable to remove the natural history collections from the British Museum and to find a home for them in Kensington. The time may come, and may not be far distant, when a further step will have to be taken in the direction of relieving the congested storehouses at Bloomsbury of some other assemblage of precious objects. In London we find ourselves more and more driven to specialize our collections, if only to save ourselves from bewilderment.

But as to any great collections of historical documents, except only that at the Record Office, they do not exist; they have still to be made. Meanwhile one large class of records—the ecclesiastical, parochial, and testamentary records—may be said to be in great danger of gradually but certainly perishing, partly from mere disuse, partly from the want of any adequate provision for their safe keeping, partly from the actual uncertainty that attaches to their ownership. One and all they are national records, the preservation of which ought to be assured to the nation by very different precautions from any which now are provided. Whom do the parish registers belong to? What guarantee have we that X or Y or Z may not sell "his" registers to the highest bidder? In point of fact, parish registers have been bought and sold again and again. Who are the owners of such a splendid collection of historic MSS. as is to be found in the archives of St. Lawrence's Church, Reading? What is to prevent the churchwardens from selling them to a "collector" and appropriating the proceeds towards the expense of a new organ? Where are the records of Barchester now that the Venerable Archdeacon Grantley has ceased to edify us with his eloquent charges? In how many instances is there to be found anything remotely resembling a catalogue of such archidiaconal records? How many living men have ever consulted such as there are or would know where to look for them?

Let me not be misunderstood. I have received so much kindness, hospitality, and cordial assistance at the hands of so many who have laid open their muniments to my inspection, I have found and made among these gentlemen such warm friends that I can only think of them and speak of them with gratitude and esteem. But who knows better than the most learned and most entirely loyal among the custodians of our ecclesiastical and parochial muniments that the state of things as they are is not the state of things that ought to be?

And yet there can surely be no insuperable difficulty in grouping together our ecclesiastical, testamentary, and parochial muniments, forming them into one homogeneous collection, and bringing them together into a single provincial record office, taking the geographical limits of the diocese as the area within which the several aggregates of ancient documents shall be deposited.

Few men can pay a visit to any of our cathedrals, especially those within whose precincts there are still to be found any considerable remains of the old conventual buildings, without being struck by what seems to be the *waste of room* in the church itself and its outlying dependencies. Not to speak of the side chapels, which some would have a sentimental objection to utilizing—though I know instances where they are mere store places for workmen's tools and lumber—consider the immense areas at our disposal in many a transept, triforium, or chapter house. Consider how comparatively small a chamber suffices, for the most part, to contain all the existing records of a cathedral chapter or of the bishop of a see. Consider how all the parochial registers even of a large diocese from 1538 to 1800 could easily stand upon a dozen shelves of ten feet long, and all the wills of two or three counties from the earliest times to the beginning of this century could be accommodated without difficulty in many a drawing-room. Consider all these things and more that I forbear from dwelling on, and it will be abundantly clear that the difficulty of providing accommodation for one group of historic MSS. at any rate will be found insignificant if we set ourselves seriously to deal with it. Within the precincts of our cathedrals there is ample space and verge enough for any such requirements as this group of records may be supposed to make upon us.

But assuming that such an assemblage, such a grouping, of historic MSS. were determined on, and that the housing of it were found to be easy and practicable, would it not be necessary that a duly qualified custodian should be appointed to take the oversight of the collection and to act as the provincial or diocesan keeper of the records? Of course it would; and this is exactly what is very urgently needed. I am told that a letter from Mr. Charles Mason, which appeared in *The Times* not so very long ago, and which gave an account of his experience in trying to institute a search among the diocesan records of Llandaff, "produced quite a sensation in some quarters." I think it must be among those who have had very little experience indeed of similar adventures. The truth is that it is the exception rather than the rule to find among the present responsible keepers of parochial testamentary or episcopal records a gentleman who even professes to be able to decipher the more ancient and precious MSS. which he has under his charge. The registrar of a diocese, of an archdeaconry, or of a prerogative court, the parson of a parish, or the churchwarden, each and all have something else to do than spend the precious hours upon poring over their muniments.

Such men as Dr. Bensley of Norwich are few and far between. Gentlemen whose duties involve many hours a day of arduous and exhausting labour can only devote their leisure moments to research, and when they do so they are in danger of getting something less than thanks as their reward. The chivalrous and splendid enthusiasm of the late Mr. Wickenden at Lincoln, of Dr. Sheppard at Canterbury, of Canon Raine at York, has laid us under profound obligation, but in each and all of these instances the labour of long years has been a labour of love, and the very permission to engage and continue in it has been conceded as a privilege conferred upon the toiler. Or again, when the fascination which "musty parchments" exercise over some minds has irresistibly impelled such generous students as Archdeacon Chapman of Ely, the late Canon Swainson of Chichester, or Mr. Symonds of Norwich, to make sacrifices of time and money in the preservation or deciphering or calendaring the precious documents to which their position as members of the chapter gave them free access, they have found some portion of their recompense in the wonder and astonishment of the Philistines that any human being could undertake and carry on so much *without being paid for it.*

A registrar is a functionary whose duty it is to keep a register of what *is* going on from day to day. I suspect it is very seldom part of his duty to find out what people were doing or recording long before he was born. At any rate it is no part of his duty to find that out for you, or to teach you where and how to look for what you want to discover. So with the parson of a parish. For the most part he is possessed by a conviction that if he loses his registers something dreadful will happen to him; and accordingly when he goes away for a holiday he leaves his cook in charge, with a solemn warning that she is to let no one see "the books" except in her presence and under her eye; and a very awful eye it sometimes is. But who of us has not been kindly and frankly told by a genial brother that if we want such or such an entry copied we must come and copy it ourselves, for that our good-natured correspondent cannot make out the old writing?

As to the churchwardens, assuming that they are to be looked upon as responsible for the custody of the parochial evidences, to talk of them as keepers of ancient MSS. is a little too ridiculous. It is true that there are in my vestry two dilapidated parish chests, which once presumably were full of wills and deeds and conveyances and evidences, which if they were now forthcoming, might considerably disturb the equanimity of some personages here and there; but those old chests are used as coal-bins now, and have been so used from times to which the memory of man doth not extend. I could tell some odd stories of my experience as a dryasdust in days when I employed my leisure hours in peeping into the dens and caves of the earth.

Assuredly if we resolve upon collecting together any group of historic MSS. and making them available for students engaged in original research, it will be necessary to put them under the custody of a trained *archiviste*, as the French call such a functionary, and give him a recognized position as provincial keeper of the records. Such an official, with one or two subordinates under him, should be required to give their time exclusively to the work marked out for them. Let that work be organized in the same way and on the same lines as those laid down in the great London *tabularium*. Let there be the same system adopted of arranging, indexing, and calendaring. Let there be issued periodically reports addressed to the central authorities, let the archives be open to students and inquirers without fee or any payment. If any one wishes to have a document transcribed or a search made which, if he knew how to set about it, he might carry on himself, let him pay for his "office copy" or his search at a reasonable charge. As for the details of such an arrangement let them settle themselves, as they surely will; in the meantime let us trust to the golden principle "Solvitur ambulando."

Can it be doubted that into such provincial depositories there would flow, in the natural course of things, a stream of contributions from the possessors of documents illustrative of county and provincial history, for which their owners have no room in their houses, which they know not how to make use of and are half inclined to burn? Nay, it will probably come to pass that collections of great historic importance will be committed for safe custody to such provincial archives on the understanding that they shall in due time be examined, arranged, and reported on, and thus the work now carried on by the Historic Manuscripts Commission will be continued in a much more exhaustive way than is now attempted by the Commissioners, who necessarily spend much of their time and much of the public money in itinerating, and whose work can only be by-work and subordinated to their daily duties and the regular business of their lives. I have known two instances of cartloads of MSS. of great antiquity, and comprehending almost certainly large numbers of charters, letters, rolls, and the like of estimable value and interest, deliberately destroyed, and in one of these instances destroyed with some difficulty and at some expense, only because they were "in the way." What I know, others doubtless may find parallels for. Would such a catastrophe have happened if there had been any recognized depository for records of this kind, which, by the very fact of their being guarded with care and intelligence and treated with respect, men had learnt to look upon as having an intrinsic value?

*　　　*　　　*　　　*　　　*

It will be noticed that in the foregoing pages I have said very little about any objections that may be urged or difficulties that may be suggested in carrying out a measure of this character.

No! I must leave that delightful duty to others. I offer a suggestion. The draughting of a *scheme* must come by-and-by. As to difficulties, sentimental, professional, or financial, we are sure to hear of them. Was there ever a proposal for any sort of reform that had not to run the gauntlet of those clamorous people who love nothing better, and are good for nothing better, than bawling out, "There's a lion in the way!"? There is no need to suggest difficulties to these people; to do so would be only to intrude into their domain. But this I am more and more convinced of, namely, that there are no difficulties in carrying out such a suggestion as is here brought forward which will not disappear if they are faced with a desire to overcome them, and I am even more convinced that a feeling is growing up in our midst against allowing the present condition of affairs to continue. It is quite sufficiently scandalous that we have submitted to it so long.

VI.
SNOWED UP IN ARCADY.

NO truer saying was ever uttered than that "one half the world does not know how the other half lives." And yet I am continually contradicted by wiseacres of the streets and squares when I meekly but firmly maintain that it is actually possible to live a happy, intelligent, useful, and *progressive* life in an out-of-the-way country parish—"far from the madding crowd"—and literally (as I happen to know at this moment) three miles from a lemon. "Don't tell me!" says one of my agnostic friends who knows everything, as agnostics always do, and who is absolutely certain, as agnostics always are, that they know all about *you*—"don't tell me! You may make the best of it as you do, and you put a good face upon it, which I dare say is all right; but to try and make me believe you *like* being buried alive is more than you can do. Stuff, man! You might as well try and persuade me you like being snowed up!"

Now it so happened that, a few days after my bouncing and aggressive friend had delivered himself of this delicate little protest against any and every assertion I might venture to make in the conversation which had arisen between us, I was awaked at the usual hour of 7 a.m. by Jemima knocking at the door; and when Mr. Bob had growled his usual growl, and I had declared myself to be awake in a surly monosyllable, Jemima cried aloud, saying, "It's awful snow, sir—drifts emendjous!" I drew the curtains open, pulled up the blinds, and lo! there was snow indeed. Not on the trees—that was well, at any rate—but all the air was full of snow. Not coming down from the clouds, but driving across the fields in billows of white dust—piling itself up against every obstacle—pollard, stump or gatepost, hedgerow, or wall, or farmstead—rolling, eddying, scudding along before the cruel north-easter, that was lashing the earth with his freezing scourge of bitterness. At about the distance of a pistol-shot from my window the high road runs straight as a ruler between low banks and thin hedges, and we can see it for half a mile or so till some rising ground blocks the view. This morning *there was no road!*—only a long broad stripe of snow that seemed a trifle higher than the ploughed lands that lay to the northward, and which were almost swept bare by the gale. To the southward there were huge drifts packed up against every little copse or plantation, and far as the eye could see not a human creature or sheep or head of cattle to lessen the impression of utter desolation.

By the time we got down to breakfast the wind had lulled, and fresh snow was falling. That was, at any rate, an improvement upon the accursed north-easter. But it was plain that there were to be no *ante-jentacular* or *post-prandial peregrinations*, as Jeremy Bentham used to phrase it, for us this day. "My dear," I said, "I'm afraid we are really snowed up!" Now, what do you suppose was the reply I received from her Royal Highness the Lady Shepherd? Neither more nor less than this—"What a jolly day we will have! We needn't go out, need we?"

Nathan, the wise youth—agnostic, as he calls himself, which is only Greek for *ignoramus*—would have sneered at the Lady Shepherd's chuckle, and she—she would have chuckled at his sneer. But as he was not there we only laughed, and somewhat gleefully set ourselves to map out the next fifteen hours with plans of operation that would have required at least fifty hours to execute.

"The only thing that can be said for your pitiful life," said Nathan to us once, "is that you have no interruptions. But there is not much in that, where there's nothing to interrupt." Nathan, the wise youth, is a type of his class. He's so delicate in his little *innuendos*, so sympathetically candid, so tender to "the things you call your feelings, you know." Do these people always wear hob-nailed boots, prepared at any moment for a wrestling match, where kicking is part of the game? "No interruptions!" Oh, Lady Shepherd, think of that! "No interruptions!"

You observe that our day begins at eight. When we came first to Arcady we said we would breakfast at half-past eight. We tried the plan for a month. It was a dead failure. Jemima never kept true to the minutes. We found ourselves slipping into nine o'clock; that meant ruin. It must either be eight o'clock, or the financial bottom of the establishment would inevitably drop out. So eight o'clock it is and shall be.

At eight o'clock, accordingly, on this particular morning we went down as usual to the library—and, I am bound to say, we were just a little depressed, because we had made up our minds that no postman in England could bring us our bag this morning. To our immense surprise and joy, there were the letters and papers lying on the table as if it were Midsummer

Day. The man had left the road, tramped along the fields which the howling wind had made passable. There were nine letters. When I see what these country postmen go through, the pluck and endurance they exhibit, the downright suffering (*i.e.*, it would be to you and me) which they take all as a part of the day's work, and how they go on at it, and retire at last, after years of stubborn jog-trotting, to enjoy a pension of ten shillings a week and the repose of acute rheumatism consequent upon sudden cessation from physical exertion, I find myself frequently exclaiming with the poet,—

πολλὰ τὰ δεινὰ κ' οὐδὲν ἀνθρώπου δεινότερον πέλει.

Many the wonderful things that be, but the wonder of wonders is—Man!

Now it will be a surprise, perhaps a very great surprise, to some of my genuine town friends, to learn that even a country parson—who after all is a man and a brother—gets pretty much the same sort of letters that other people do. He gets offers to assign to him shares in gold mines; offers of three dozen and four, positively all that is left, of that transcendental sherry; offers to make him a life governor of the new college for criminals; invitations to be a steward at a public dinner of the Society for Diminishing Felony; above all, he gets some very elegant letters from gentlemen in very high positions in society offering to lend him money. I do verily believe these scoundrels, who invariably write a good hand on crested paper and express themselves in a style which is above all praise, are in league with one of my banker's clerks. How else does it happen that, as sure as ever my account is very low and that I am in mortal terror lest my last cheque should be returned dishonoured, so sure am I to hear from one of these diabolical tempters? There's one scarlet Mephistopheles who *must* know all about my financial position. How else could he have thought of sending me two of his gilt-edged seductions in a single week just when my banking account was overdrawn? It is absurd to pretend that he keeps a *medium*.

Moreover, proof sheets come by post even in this wilderness, and they have to be corrected, too; and real letters that are not begging letters come, some kind and comforting, some stern and uncompromising, some with the oddest inquiries and criticisms. Sometimes, too, anonymous letters come. What a queer state of mind a man must have got himself into before he can sit down to write an anonymous letter! Does any man in his senses ever *read* an anonymous letter of four pages? If he does, the *writer* gets no fun out of it. I am inclined to think that the practice of writing anonymous letters is dying out now that the schoolmaster is abroad; and yet, they tell me, insanity is not decreasing. Then, too, there are the newspapers. I could live without butter—I shouldn't like it, but I could submit to it; or without eggs, though I dislike snow pancakes; or without sugar—and there are some solids and some liquids that are insipid without that; but there is one thing I could not do without—I could not do without the *Times*. We have tried again and again to economize by having a penny paper, but it has always ended in the same way. As *entremets* they are all delightful, but for a square meal give me the *Times*. Without it "the appetite is distracted by the variety of objects, and tantalized by the restlessness of perpetual solicitation," till, when the day is done, the mind wearies under "a feeling of satiety without satisfaction, and of repletion without sustenance."

On this particular morning we had adjourned from the library to the breakfast-room, and were opening our letters in high spirits, spite6 of Nathan the wise, and notwithstanding the bitter wind and the snow, when a hideous sound startled us. There, under the window, the snow steadily falling, drawn up in single file, were four human creatures, two males and two females, arrayed in outlandish attire, and every one of them playing hideously out of tune. It was a German band!

A more lugubrious spectacle than is presented by a German band, droning forth "Herz, mein Herz" in front of your window in a snowstorm it would be difficult to imagine. We suffer much from German bands, but we have only ourselves to thank. I love music, and I am possessed by the delusion that it is my duty to encourage the practice of instrumental execution. Five or six years ago there was a band of eight or nine performers who perambulated Norfolk, and they came to me at least once a month. Whenever they appeared I went out to them and gave them a shilling, airing my small modicum of German periodically, and receiving flattering compliments upon my pronunciation, which gratified me exceedingly. These people disappeared at last, but they were succeeded by another band, and a very inferior one, and I took but little notice of them. There were seven of these performers, a cornet and two clarionets being prominent—very. However, they got their shilling, and vanished. Three days after their departure came another band: this time there were only four. I thought that rather shabby, but I was busy, did not take much notice of them, and again gave them a shilling. The cornet player was really quite respectable. Next day came four more, and there was no cornet, only the abominable clarionet. It was insufferable. I said I really must restrict myself to sixpence, and that was fourpence more than they were worth. Two days after their departure came a single solitary performer; he had a pan-pipe fastened under his chin, a peal of bells on his head, which he caused to tinkle by his nods, a pair of cymbals attached to his elbows, a big drum which he beat by the help of a crank that he worked with one of his feet, and a powerful concertina which he played with his hands. He led off with a dolorous chorale in a minor key. It was really more than flesh and blood could bear. "Send him away, Jemima. Send him away!—instantly! Tell him I am *sehr krank*. Send him away!" The fellow smiled with unctuous complacency. But when he got only twopence, his face fell. "Ach, nein! You plaize, ze professor, he geeve one sheeling to ze band—I am ze band. He geeve ze band only twopence. He do not understand I am ze band! You plaise tell him I am ze band!" "No! You're to go away. Master's sore and kranky!" Ze band loitered for half a minute; then it took itself to pieces and went its way. But the fellow's hint about the shilling was significant, and led to an investigation. Then it turned out that the band of seven or eight which was going its rounds that year, split itself up when it came into my neighbourhood, and, in view of my shilling, presented itself in two detachments, each of which reckoned on my shilling, and several times carried it off. Now I give one penny for each performer, and only when there is a cornet do I send out coffee to the instrumentalists.

It was, however, not in flesh and blood to withhold the shilling from the players of that quartette on that bitter morning. It was heart-rending to think of their having at the peril of their lives staggered through three miles of snowdrifts. It was inhuman to send them away without coffee. And they had it accordingly. Poor things! poor things! Where were they going? They were going back to the "Red Lion," a stone's throw off, where they had slept the night before, and where they meant to spend this night in delighting the hearts of the rustics by waltzes and polkas, and gathering not such a bad harvest for the nonce.

"Lor, sir!" said Mr. Style, "to hear that there trombone a *soléing* 'Rule Britannia'! That made you feel he was a real musician— that it did!"

So you see we began the day with a band of music. That does not sound so bad. But the band being dismissed, we finish our breakfast and retire to the library.

We do not go empty-handed. Each of us carries a plate piled up high with bread cut up for the birds that are waiting to be fed. A space under the window is swept clear from snow, and there the birds are, ready for their breakfast. Sparrows by the score, robins that will hardly wait till the window is opened, chaffinches and tomtits, dunnocks, blackbirds and thrushes, linnets and—jackdaws, yes! and, watching very warily for a chance, a dozen or so of rooks in the trees in yonder plantation, very much excited, very restless, very shy, but ready to come down and gobble up the morsels if we keep ourselves out of sight. As to the robins, there is no *mauvaise honte* about them; they will almost fly on to the plate. Sometimes I send a shower of morsels quite over the robins, and they greatly enjoy the fun. One saucy little fellow last week laughed out loud at me. "Laughed?" Yes, laughed! I've known a robin laugh convulsively. But then it was not under a street lamp.

It is one of the laws of this palace that we do not begin real work before half-past nine. And before that time arrives there is usually a good half-hour for reading aloud by the Lady Shepherd. What is the Shepherd doing meanwhile? He is not going to tell you anything more than this, that he is devoting himself during that half-hour to preventing the ravages of moths and bookworms. You people who suppose we poor country folk must be horribly dull and depressed may as well understand that this library in which I am sitting is an apartment that for a country parsonage may be regarded as palatial. Pray haven't I a right to have one good room in my house? One thing I know, and that is that I am rated as if I lived in a house of £430 a year, and if I must pay rates on that amount I may as well have something to show for it. Also I would have you to know that the walls of this library are lined with books from floor to ceiling. Then there are flowers all about—grown on the premises, mind you—none of your bought blossoms stuck on to a bit of stick with a bit of wire, but live flowers that turn and look at you—at any rate, they certainly do turn and look out at the window if you give them a chance. Moreover, they are not under the dominion of a morose stipendiary, for the sufficient reason that the head gardener is the Lady Shepherd, and the under gardener only comes three times a week, and Jabez has his hands full, and Ishmael is no servant of ours, but the servant of the maids in the kitchen; and when you're snowed up Ishmael must give his life to the solemn duties of a stoker and filler of coal-scuttles, and to shovelling away the snow, and to running errands. There is no doubt about the seriousness of that boy. He is oppressed by the sense of his responsibility, and convinced that he occupies the position of the divine being in Plato's *Theætetus*. As long as τὸ ὄν kept his hand upon the world it went round all right; when he took it off, the world straightway spun round the wrong way. That being Ishmael's view, he is naturally grave. When the maids shriek at him he exhibits a terror-stricken alacrity, but when I tell him to do this or that, he looks at me with a cunning expression as if he would say, "Do you really mean that? Well, you must take the consequences." Then he glides off. From Ishmael not much is to be expected in the greenhouse. But when half-past nine strikes I roll my table into position and set to work, my head gardener puts on her apron and gathers up her skirts, and starts forth with her basket on her arm, equipped for *her* day's work.

Now, if a man has four good hours in the morning which he may call his own, it's a great deal more than most men have, and there's no saying what may be done in such hours as these. But if you allow morning callers to disturb you, then it's—I was going to say a bad word!

I had just settled myself to work in earnest when Jemima's head appeared. "Please, sir, Tinker George wants to see you." "Tell your mistress." And I thought no more about it, but went on with what I was doing. If Tinker George had been one of my parishioners I should have jumped up and heard him patiently, but Tinker George does not belong to me, but to the next parish, and as his usual object in coming to see me is to show me his poetry, I passed him on this time, knowing very certainly that he would not be the worse for my not seeing him. An hour later I got up to warm myself. "May I speak?" said the Lady Shepherd. "I let Tinker George go away, but I'm afraid you'll be sorry I did. I think you would have liked to see him." "What's the matter?" "He's been writing to the dear Queen" (the Lady Shepherd always speaks of "the *dear* Queen") "and he came to show you the letter, and to ask what address he should put on it."

Tinker—George—writing to—the—Queen! What *did* the man want? He wanted to be allowed to keep a dog without paying tax for it. George goes about with a wheel, and he calls for broken pots and pans. Sometimes he finds the boys extremely annoying, they will persist in turning his wheel when his back is turned and he has gone into a house for orders. Now, you see, if he had a dog of spirit and ferocity chained to his wheel, George might leave that wheel in charge of that dog; but then a dog is an expensive luxury when there is the initial outlay of seven shillings and sixpence for the tax. So he wrote to the Queen, and he put it into the post, and I never saw it. This was just one of those things which cause a man lifelong regret, all the more poignant because so vain. The Lady Shepherd is the most passionately loyal person in England, and she firmly believes that there will come a holograph reply from her Majesty in the course of a few days addressed to Tinker George, promptly and graciously granting him his very reasonable request. "I've promised Tinker George," she added, "to give him a sovereign for the letter when it comes, and it shall have a box all to itself among my autographs."

Be pleased to observe that it was only just noon, and two events of some interest had happened already, though we were snowed up. But at this point I must needs inform you who *we* are. In the first place there are the Shepherd and the Lady Shepherd; in the second place there are the Shepherd's dogs. No shepherd can live without dogs—it would not be safe. No *man* ever pulled another man out of the snow: it is perfectly well known that men don't know how to do it. Till lately we had three of these protectors. But—*eheu fugaces!*—we have only two now; one a blue Skye, silky, surly, and exceptionally stubborn; and a big colley, to whom his master is the Almighty and the All-wise. I do not wish to claim more for my friends than is due to them. Ours are only average dogs; but they *are* average dogs. And if any one will have the hardihood to assert that he holds the average man to be equal to the average dog in morals, manners, and intelligence, I will not condescend to argue with that purblind personage. I will only say that he knows no more about dogs than I do about moles, and I never kept a tame mole.

Nothing perplexes some of my friends more than to hear that I do not belong to a single London club. Not belong to a club? One man was struck dumb at the intelligence; he looked at me gravely—suspicion in every wrinkle of his face, perplexity in the very buttons of his waistcoat. He was working out the problem mentally. I saw into his brain. I almost heard him say to himself, "Not belong to a club? Holloa! Ever been had up for larceny? Been a bankrupt? Wonder why they all blackballed him?—give it up!" He evidently wanted to ask what it meant—there must be something wrong which he did not like to pry into: a skeleton in the cupboard, in fact.

"I said a *London* club!" I added, to relieve his embarrassment. "Of course I do belong to a club *here*—the Arcadian Club. It's a very select club, too, and we can introduce strangers, which is an advantage, as you may perhaps yourself have felt if you have ever been kept for ten minutes stamping on the door-mat of the Athenæum with the porter watching you while that arch boy was sauntering about, pretending to carry your card to your friend upstairs. We are rational beings in our club, and I'll introduce you at once—Colonel Culpepper, Toby! Colonel Culpepper, Mr. Bob." Neither Toby nor Mr. Bob took the least notice of the gallant colonel, who seemed rather shy himself. "They're dangerous dogs are colleys, so I'm told. In London it does not so much matter, because, you see, they must go about with a muzzle. And this is really all the club you belong to?"

Yes. This and no other; the peculiarities of our club being that false witness, lying, and slandering were never so much as known among the members. There is a house dinner every day, music every evening, no sneering, no spite, no gossip, no entrance fee, no annual subscription, no blackballing, no gambling, no betting, and no dry champagne or dry anything. Show me a club like that, my dear colonel, and I'll join it to-morrow, whether in Pall Mall or in the planet Jupiter. At the present moment I know of only one such club, and it is here—the Arcadian Club! Enjoy its privileges while you may, and be grateful.

Seriously, I defy any club in England or anywhere else to produce me fifty per cent. of its members so entirely courteous, cordial, and clubbable—so graceful, intelligent, and generous—such thorough gentlemen, and so entirely guiltless of talking nonsense, as our friends Toby and Mr. Bob. Of course there are the infirmities which all flesh is heir to, and jealousy is one of these. But put the case that you should say to a little *man*, "You may sleep inside that door on a cushion by the fire," and say to a big *man*, "You're to sleep outside that same door on the mat!" and put the case that each of those *men* knew he was a member of the same club to which the fire, the cushion, and the mat belonged:—and pray what *modus vivendi* could be found between the big *man* and the little *man* on this side the grave?

But to return. The snow had ceased falling, but in the bleak distance as far as the eye could see, the road was blocked by ugly-looking drifts, in which a man on horseback might very easily be buried and flounder hopelessly till he sank exhausted never to rise again. There was nothing stirring except the birds, looking fluffy, cold, and starving. So I turned my chair to my table again and resumed my task.

Hark! Actually a ring at the front-door bell. The dogs growled and sniffed, but there was no fierce barking. Confound these tramps! That trombone has gone back to the "Red Lion," and the rogues are oozing out to practise upon our weakness. "That's not a tramp," said the Lady Shepherd. "Toby didn't bark." She was right, as she always is. For Toby has quite an unerring discernment of the proximity of a tramp. His gift in this line is inexplicable. How the great Darwin would have delighted to observe that dog! If it was not a tramp, who could it be? "I believe it's Polus!" said the Lady Shepherd. "Only Polus could have the ferocity to come here in defiance of the snowdrifts." Right again. It *was* Polus. She had given him the name because he was eager to get into the County Council.— Poor man! He only got three votes.—There was no reference to the young gentleman in the *Gorgias* who bore that name— only a desire to indicate that he was the man who *went to the Poll*.

It was hardly more than noon; we were snowed up, and yet already we had had music; poetry as represented by Tinker George; a flood of literature; and now there was discussion imminent on the profoundest questions of politics, philosophy, and law.

Enter Polus! What in the world had brought him hither this dreadful day? What had he been doing? whither was he going? Should we put him to bed? To send for a doctor was out of the question. But we could soon get him a mustard poultice and a hot bath. Polus laughed the hearty laugh of rude health and youth. "You, dear old people, you forget I'm only thirty-five. I've had a pleasant walk from Tegea—greased my boots well—only rolled over twice. I've come for a talk. Dear me! dear me! Didn't I see a moth there on the curtains? Curious that they should come out in such numbers when you're snowed up! May I help you to get rid of the pests?"

The man had come to show his defiance of the laws of nature and ordinary prudence. In fact, he had come for mere *cussedness*! Also he had come for a conference. What was the subject to be this time? "Anything but the education question," said I; "we must draw the line somewhere. Woman's rights, Man's wrongs. Agricultural depression. The People's Palace. The Feudal System. The Bacon-Shakespeare—anything you please in reason—but Education! No! Not for worlds." It was not long before the cat jumped out of the bag. Polus was bent on floating a most magnificent new International League. His ideas were a trifle mixed, but so are those of many men in our times. Polus makes the mistake of *bottling* his grand schemes and laying them down, as it were, when they ought to be kept *on draught*. The result is that there's always a superabundance of froth—or shall we call it foam?—that we have to plunge into before we can taste of that pleasant draught; and when you have drunk about half your fill, there's a wholly unnecessary and somewhat disagreeable sediment at the bottom, which interferes with your enjoyment. Thus the new League was to be so comprehensive a League, for effecting so many desirable objects, that it was difficult to discover what the main object was—or, in fact, if the main object did not resolve itself into an assemblage of objects, each of which was struggling with the rest for prominence and supremacy.

On this occasion Polus had the effrontery to begin by assuring me that I was in honour and conscience bound to join the League, for the idea of it had been first suggested to him by a pregnant and suggestive saying of mine some months before. "What! when you were so hot for the abolition of the punishment by death?" Oh dear no. He'd changed his mind about that long ago. "Was it when you were advocating the desirability of the labourers having the cows and the landlords keeping the land?" "No, no! I've improved greatly upon that. Haven't you heard? I'm for letting the landlord keep the cows, but giving the labourers the calves only; that appears to me the equitable adjustment of a complex question." I thought a little, and Polus gave me time. What was it? What could it have been that we had been talking about? Enfantin's hullucinations and the dual priesthood (*couple-prêtre*)? Fourrier's Phalanstery? It must have been an *obiter dictum* which dropped from me as he laid down the law about Proudhon. I shook my head. "Don't you remember? Entails!"

Then it appeared that the great League was to be started for the abolition of everything in the shape of entails. In our last conference I had let fall the remark that for every acre of land tied up in strict entail there was a thousand pounds sterling tied up in much stricter entail. If you are going to deal with the one, why not with the other? Polus was putting on his hat when I gave him that parting dig, and I thought I had silenced him for ever. So far from it, I had but sown a new seed in his soul, and now he came to show me the baby.

Polus meanwhile had plunged into the heaving billows of statistics. He had discovered, to his own satisfaction, that 500 millions of the National Debt was strictly entailed; that 217 millions belonged prospectively to babes unborn; that the British people were paying "enormous taxes, sir!" not only for the sins and extravagances of their forefathers, but for enriching of their hypothetical progeny. That it was a state of things altogether outrageous, irrational, monstrous, and a great many other epithets. Would I join the League? Of course I'd join a league for the extinction of nasal catarrh or the annihilation of stupidity—gladly, but upon conditions. I must first know how the thing is to be effected. Your object may be heroic, but the means for carrying out this glorious reform? the machinery, my dear Polus? Let me hear more about *that*. A new *voyage en Icarie* implies that you are going to embark upon some safe vessel. By the way, how did Cabet get to his enchanting island?

Hereupon ensued an elaborate monologue, admirably expressed, closely reasoned, carrying not so much conviction as demonstration along with it. Granting the premises, the conclusion was inevitable. It was as good as Bishop Blougram. The scheme was this: Property—even in the funds—is a fact. There is no denying that. Therefore face the facts first, and deal with them as such. Timid reformers go only halfway towards building up the ideal social fabric. They say meekly, nationalize the land. The true reformer says, abolish all permanent financial obligations. But hardships would ensue upon any sudden and violent extinction of *private* debts. Prudence suggests that you should begin by a gradual extinction of *public* debts—in other words, the National Debt. The living holders of stock shall be fairly dealt with, and during their lifetime they shall enjoy their abominable dividends wrenched from the pockets of the people. As they drop off—and the sooner they go the better—their several claims upon the tax-payer shall perish with them. None shall succeed to their privileges of robbing the teeming millions. All stock standing in the name of trustees shall be transferred to the names of the present beneficiaries, and shall be extinguished by the death of the several holders. All powers of bequest in regard of such stock shall be taken away. In the case of infants—and there are 147,623 of such cases—who are only prospective owners of stock—being *only* prospective owners, and therefore having never actually tasted the joys of unrighteous possession—they shall continue to be prospective owners, and never be allowed to become anything else. They will have nothing to complain of; you take from them nothing that they ever had. All that will happen to them will be that they will be saved from cherishing delusive hopes, such as should never have been aroused in them. The scales will drop from their eyes; they will no longer be the victims of treacherous phantasms. The sooner they learn their glorious lesson the better. They will speedily rise to a true conception of the dignity of citizenship, and grow to the stature of a loftier humanity, whose destiny who shall foreshadow? "Now, my dear Doctor," said Polus, pausing for a moment in his harangue, "I ask you as a Christian and a philosopher, is not ours a magnificent League, and is not the vision that opens before us sublime?"

"Place aux dames! Place aux dames!" I answered. "Ask the Lady Shepherd. Let her speak."

*   *   *   *   *

It is a curious physiological fact that I have been puzzled by for several years past, and which I am only half able to explain or account for, that *flashing* eyes have almost disappeared from off the face of the earth. You may see many sorts of eyes—eyes of various shades of colour and various shapes—eyes that glitter, that gleam, that sparkle, that shine, that stare, that blink; even eyes that are guilty of the vulgarity of winking; but eyes that flash with the fire and flame of wrath, and scorn, and scorching indignation—such as once or twice I have cowered and trembled under when I was young—such eyes have passed away; the passion in them has been absorbed in something, it may be better or it may be worse—absorbed in utter tenderness. The last time I saw eyes flash was when a certain college don came to pay his respects to a certain little lady—she *was* a little lady then—a week after she was married. The old blunderer boasted that he had been on Lord Powis's committee on a certain memorable occasion. "Ah, my dear madam, you are too young to know anything about that, and your husband of course was an undergraduate. But——" The man almost jumped from his chair; he turned pale as an oyster. The little lady sprang up a pillar of flame. "Do you mean, sir, that you voted against the Prince Consort? You will oblige me by not referring to the subject." I rang the bell again and again; I called for buckets of water—the whole room seemed to be, the whole house seemed likely to be on fire.

Ah! there were real live Tories (spelt with a capital T) then. We were blue *or* yellow, not a pale green made up by smudging the two together. We didn't stand upon legs that were not a pair. None of your Conservative Liberals or Liberal Conservatives going about hat in hand and timidly asking, "What will you be good enough to wish to have conserved?" It was "Church and Queen, sir, or salt and water. No shilly-shallying." Hesitate, and nothing remained for you but pistols for two in the back yard. Argument? Nay! We dealt with that as Uncle Sammy's second wife did, and everyone knows that

She with the heel of assertionStampt all his arguments down!

If I could have looked forward in those days, what a monster would my future self have appeared!

Tempora mutantur nos et mutamur in illis.

*   *   *   *   *

Something in the look of the Lady Shepherd's, eyes this snowy morning reminded me of the old terrible flash; but it all passed, and only merriment shone out. "Sublime, my good Polus? How can a vision be sublime? A visionary is at best a dreamer, and a vision is a sham. A sublime sham is a contradiction in terms. Why don't you try and talk sense sometimes?" "You're not a bit better than that chit of a girl with a mop on her head

that came gabbling here last week. But it's like you men—
you've no more common sense than this trowel! Visions
indeed!

I gladly live amid the real,
And I seek a worthier ideal.
Courage, brothers; God is overhead!

Ah! you may laugh. But it's all on my side."

Away she swept, basket and trowel and all. Stop to listen to
that gibberish—not she!

When her Royal Highness came back to us [in these moods
she is the Princess, in her gentler and more pastoral moods she
is the Lady Shepherd] she found us deep in another part of the
discussion. The business of the Great International League
having extinguished the National Debt by a very simple
process, the next stall in the Augean stable of existing
abomination, as he expressed it, must be dealt with. "Suppose
we change the metaphor, my dear Polus, and say the next plank
in your platform must be pulled up." "Pulled up? Quite the
contrary. Fixed, firmly fixed, nailed down!" "Be it so! Let us
look at the plank. A stall in the stable of abominations suggests
dirty work, you know!"

The next great problem which the Great International League
sets before itself to solve is this: the National Debt being
annihilated, how is the accumulation of property to be
prevented in the future? I observed that at this point Polus was
not so inclined for the monologue form of discussion as
before. It was not the Socratic speaking *ex cathedrâ*, as in the
Laws; there was a quite unusual glad-of-a-hint attitude, as in the
Lysis or the *Meno*.

"Come," I said, "I see through you; you haven't thought it out,
and you want me to give you a hint. Which is it to be? Am I to
serve as whetstone, or do you come in trouble and pain crying
out for τὴν μαιείαν?" He threw up his hands: "Speak, and I will
listen." Then said I, "O Polus, you're just the man I want.
Everybody knows I am a dull old dog, slow of thought and
slow of speech as a country bumpkin must be; feeling after my
words, and as often as not choosing the wrong ones. But I have
been excogitating of late a theory which will supply your next
plank to perfection, and in fact would make your fortune as a
politician, if indeed the Great League will allow you to have

any property, even in your brains. Forty years ago—for there were *thinkers*, my dear Polus, in the waste places of the earth even before you were born—I came across quite a "sublime" scheme of some French financier, propounded, I think, during the Great Revolution, for which the world was not yet ready. The man was before his age, and his own generation pooh-poohed him. I quite forget his name. I quite forget the title of his book if he ever wrote one; and I shall be very much obliged to you if you can find out something about the great man, for a great man he was. When I heard of this scheme I was little more than a lad, and now, after much cogitation, I cannot honestly tell you how much of the plan is his and how much my own. But I'll give him all the credit for it."

The scheme was a scheme for automatically adjusting all incomes and reducing them to something like equilibrium—that is, the operation of the process set in motion would tend in that direction. All incomes, no matter from what sources derived, were to be fixed according to an algebraic formula, and the formula was this:

$\cdot 0001 \ (x\text{-}m)^2$ = The income tax levied upon each citizen.

Here x=the actual income earned by the citizen;

m=1,000 pounds sterling, or an equivalent in francs or dollars, if you prefer it.

When x=m, then of course there could be nothing to pay; which is only another way of saying that a man with £1,000 a year was free from all taxation.

When x was greater than m, then taxation upon the income in excess of £1,000 came into operation with rather alarming rapidity: until when a man was convicted of having in any single year made £10,000 his taxation amounted to £8,100 for that year, and if he were ever found guilty of having made an income of £12,000 the State claimed the whole in obedience to this great and beneficent law.

But what happens in the case of those who have an income below the £1,000 a year—that is, when x is less than m?

In this case the grandeur and sagacity, not to speak of the paternal character of the scheme, become apparent. The moment a man begins to earn more than the normal £1,000 a year, that moment he begins to pay his beautifully adjusted quota of taxation to the State; but the moment that his income falls below the £1,000, that moment the State begins to pay him. Of course you will not forget that *minus* into *minus* gives *plus*, therefore the square of the *minus* quantity represented by x-m, where m is greater than x, offers no difficulty. The two poles of this perfect sphere, if I may so speak, this financial orb—*teres atque rotundus*—are reached, first when x=0, last when x = £11,000. In the first case the State comes to the help of the pauper who has earned or can earn nothing, and gives him a ten-thousandth part of a hypothetical million, which amounts to exactly £100 a year; in the other case the State deprives the bloated plutocrat of a ten-thousandth part of the same million, and relieves the dangerous citizen of ten thousand out of the eleven, saying to him, "Citizen, be grateful that you still have your thousand, and beware how you persist in piling up riches, for the State knows how to gather them."

"Now, my dear Polus, next time you come, do bring me tidings of my Frenchman, and do work the thing out on paper, for I never was much of a mathematician, and now my decimals are scandalously vague!" So Polus went his way with a dainty rosebud in a dainty paper box for Mrs. Polus, and a saucy message from the Lady Shepherd. "Tell her, with my love, I'm very sorry her husband's such a goose!" We watched him floundering through the snowdrifts; and I verily believe he was working out my problem with his stick, ·0001 $(x-m)^2$.

I don't think that man went away much impressed with the darkness and desolation of our Arcadian life. Nay, I'm inclined to think the other side had something to say, and I'm afraid this is what it said: "Oh yes, it's all very fine—intellectual intercourse, and so on. Freshens you up? Glad to see people? Of course I am. But I *did* hope we were going to have a long day together, and there! it's all broken into. It's always the way. How was I to do my autographs with him extinguishing my £1,000 in the funds all the while?"

      *   *   *   *   *

Here I may as well explain that the Shepherd and his lady are the objects of some wonder and perplexity to their great friends on the one hand and their little friends on the other. The first pronounce them to be poor as rats; the second declare that they are rolling in riches. This conflict of opinion is easily accounted for. When the great and noble Asnapper comes to smile at us he has to take pot-luck. Come when he may, there is all due provision—

Ne turpe toral, ne sordida mappa
Corruget nares, ne non et cantharus et lanx
Ostendat tibi te.

But the forks are all electro-plate, and the dishes are all of the willow pattern. When meek little Mr. Crumb brings Mrs. Crumb and two of the eight daughters to enjoy one hearty meal at afternoon tea, he is awe-struck by the sight of the books and the splendour of half a dozen good engravings hanging upon the walls. As the old grey pony trots home in high spirits—for Jabez has a standing order always to give that poor little beast a double feed of corn—Mr. Crumb remarks to Mrs. Crumb, "Those people must be extremely affluent. I wonder he does not restore his church!"

The great and noble Asnapper, on the contrary, observes, "All the signs of deep poverty, my dear. Keeps his pluck up, though. Quite out of character with the general appearance of the establishment to have those books and collections and what not. I suppose some uncle left him the things. Cooking? I forgot to notice that; but the point of one's knife went all sorts of ways, and the earthenware was most irritating. Eccentric people. The Lady Shepherd, as they call her, has actually got near a thousand autographs. Why in the world doesn't she send them up to Sotheby's and buy some new stair carpets?" Ah! why indeed? Because such as she and the Shepherd have a way of their own which is not exactly your way, my noble Asnapper; because they have made their choice, and they do not repent it. Some things they have, and take delight in them; some things they have not, and they do without them.

But not even in Arcady is it all cakes and ale. Thank God we have our duties as well as our enjoyments; pursuits and tastes we have, and the serious blessed duties which call us from excess in self-indulgence. When the roads are blocked for man and beast we chuckle because there can be no obligation to trudge down to the school a mile and a half off, or to go and pay that wedding call upon the little bride who was married last week, or to inquire about the health of Mrs. Thingoe on the common, whose twins are ten days old.

But snow or no snow, as long as old Biddy lives, one of us positively must go and look after "the old lady." Every man, woman, and child in the parish calls her "the old lady," and a real old lady she is. Biddy was ninety-three last November. She persists she's ninety-four—"leastways *in* my ninety-four. That Register only said when I was christened, you know, and who's a-going to say how long I was born before I was christened?"

Biddy has been married three times, and she avers that she wouldn't mind marrying again if she could get another partner equal to her second. Every one of her husbands had had one or more wives before he wedded Biddy. We make out that Biddy and her three spouses committed an aggregate of twelve acts of matrimony. If you think that old Biddy is a feeble old dotard, drivelling and maundering, you never made a greater mistake in your life. She is as bright as a star of the first magnitude, and as shrewd as the canniest Scotchman that ever carried a pack. She is almost the only genuine child of Arcady I ever knew who has a keen sense of humour, and is always on the look-out for a joke. She is quite the only one in whom I have noticed any tender pity for the fallen, not because of the consequences that followed the lapse, but simply and only because it was a fall. Biddy lives by herself in a house very little bigger than an enlarged dog-kennel, and much smaller than an average cow-house. Till she was eighty-three she went about the country with a donkey and cart, hawking; since then she has managed to exist, and pay her rent too, on eighteen pence a week and a stone of flour. She is always neat and clean, and more than cheerful. She has been knitting socks for me for eight years past, and I am provided with sufficient hosiery now to last me even to the age of the patriarchs. Of course we demoralise old Biddy; her little home is hardly 100 yards off the parsonage, and every now and then the old lady comes to tea in the kitchen. One of the servants goes to fetch her, and another takes her home; and, as I have said, most days one of us goes to sit with her, and I make it a rule never to leave her without making her laugh. You may think what you like, but I hold that innocent merriment keeps people healthy in mind and body, improves the digestion, clears the intellect, brightens the conscience, prepares the soul for adoration—for is not gaiety the anticipation of that which in the spiritual world will be known as fulness of joy?

On this day of snow I found Biddy sitting before the fire, half expecting me and half doubting whether I could get there. "'Cause, you know, you ain't as young as you was when you came here first." "Is any one, Biddy?" She looked up in her sly way. "Dash it, I ain't!" By her side on the little table was a Book of Common Prayer in very large print, and her spectacles on it. "I've begun to read that book through," she said, "and I've got as far as where it's turned down, but there's some on it as I've got to be very particular with. That there slanting print, that's hard, that is; that ain't so easy as the rest on it. But I'm going to read it all through for all that. You see I've *done* it all before, and some of it comes easy." "Well, Biddy, you ought to know the marriage service by this time." "And so I do," said Biddy, grinning. "But I never had no churchings, and I don't hold wi' that there *Combination*. Dash it! I never did like cussing and swearing!"7 It turned out that Biddy had set herself the task of reading the Prayer Book through, *rubrics and all*. Very funny, wasn't it? Pray, my reverend brethren of the clergy, have you all of you set yourselves the same task and carried it out?

A little later the Lady Shepherd dropped in to look at Biddy. She found the old woman chuckling over some very mild pleasantry of mine, which she repeated in her own odd way. Suddenly she stopped. "Our doctor won't live to ninety-four!" "Oh, Biddy, that's more than you can tell. One thing is quite certain; if he does, you won't be here to see him." "Why sha'n't I?" answers Biddy. "He's nigh upon threescore, ain't he? and I'm in my ninety-four. You can't tell, neither, as I shan't be here. The Lord knows."

*   *   *   *   *

Dear old Biddy! Who *does* know anything? It seems to me that we can none of us know anything about anything but the past. I hardly know whether we are most ignorant of the things that shall be or the things that are. Old Biddy is the last of the old-world folk that fascinated me so much with their legends and traditions and reminiscences when first I settled among them—it seems but yesterday. Old Biddy has told me all she has to tell, the gossip and the experiences of days that were not as our days. With her will pass away all that is left of a generation that was the generation of our fathers. If I leave her with a smile upon the wrinkled old face there is more often a shade of sadness that passes over my own. Other faces rise up before me; other voices seem to sound; the touch of the vanished hand—gone—gone! As I turn homeward with bowed head in the grey twilight, and muse upon those ten years that have rushed by so peacefully, and yet which have remorselessly levied their tribute and left me beggared of some who were dearer than all the jewels of the mine—

The farm-smokes, sweetest sight on earth,
Slow through the winter air a-shrinking,
Seem kind o' sad, and round the hearth
Of empty places set me thinking.

That, however, is not because Arcady is Arcady, but because life is life.

Such as we have long ago found the secret of contentment, and something more. Shall I tell you what that secret is? Will you promise to take it as the rule of your own life if I do? Here it is, then, wrapped up in a very short and pithy aphorism—"The man who does not like the place he *has to live in* is a fool." Ponder it well, you people who are never tired of prescribing "a change" as absolutely necessary to endurable existence. Banished to the sweetest village in England, how dazed and forlorn you'd be! *We* could accommodate ourselves to your life as easily as we could put on a new suit of clothes. *You* could never accommodate yourselves to ours. You would mope and pine. Your only solace would be in droning forth a new version of the *Tristia*, which would not be half as melodious as Ovid's.

This poor Shepherd and his Lady Shepherd will never see the Alps again—never take a boat on Lugano's lake in the summer evening, never see Rome or Florence, never again stand before the Sistine Madonna, hearing their hearts beat. Ravenna will remain for them unvisited, and Munich will be welcome to keep its acres of splashes, which Britain's young men and maidens are told with some insistence are genuine works of Rubens, every one of them. These are joys of the past. But if you assume that two old fogies like us *must* be longing for a change, fidgeting and hankering after it, and that we *must* be getting rusty, dull, and morose for lack of it, that we are eating our hearts out with a querulous whimpering, instead of brimming over with thankfulness all day and every day—then you do us grievous wrong. What, sir! Do you take us for a couple of babies floundering in a tub, and puling for a cake of Pears' Soap? Arcady or Athens is much the same to us. Where our home must be, there are our hearts.

NOTE.
THE AUTOMATIC ADJUSTMENT OF INCOMES.

This—the great financial measure of the future—can hardly be expected to commend itself to the philosophic economists of the present day. It is the penalty which every man who is before his time must expect to pay for his excessive sagacity, that his contemporaries neglect or deride him. Accordingly the very name of the French thinker who suggested this beautiful scheme for ensuring Liberty, Equality, and Fraternity has been forgotten and—will it be believed?—the number of those who have ever taken the trouble to work out his formula is quite disgracefully small.

The *Formula* of the great unknown stands thus:—

$\cdot 0001\ (\mathbf{x} - \mathbf{m})^2$ = The amount which the state deals with in all incomes above £100 a year.8

Here $\mathbf{x}$ = the income. $\mathbf{m}$ = £1,000.

In working out this Formula, the *Rule* may be stated as follows:—

1. From the number of pounds of income ($\mathbf{x}$) deduct 1,000.

2. Multiply the remainder into itself, *i.e.*, *square* it.

3. Divide the product by 10,000.

The result will give—

(i) The amount paid *by* the State to the owners of income *under* £1,000 a year.

(ii) The amount paid *to* the State by owners of income *above* £1,000 a year.

Examples:—

(*a*) Income of £200 a year; *i.e.*, $\mathbf{x}$ = 200.

200 - 1,000 = -800.
-800 squared; [*i.e.*,-800 multiplied by -800] = 640,000.

Result of 640,000/10,000 = 64.

Consolation income to all possessors of £200 a year ... £64.

(*b*) Income of £500 a year; *i.e.*, $\mathbf{x}$ = 500.

500 - 1,000 = -500.
-500 squared; [*i.e.*,-500 multiplied by -500] = 250,000.

Result of 250,000/10,000 = 25.

Consolation income to all possessors of £500 a year ... £25.

(*c*) Income of £900 a year; *i.e.*, **x** = 900.

900 - 1,000 = -100.
-100 squared; [*i.e.*, -100 multiplied by -100] = 10,000.

Result of 10,000/10,000 = 1.

Consolation income to all possessors of £900 a year ... £1.

(*d*) Income of £1,000 a year; *i.e.*, **x** = 1,000.

1,000 - 1,000 = 0.
0 multiplied by 0 = 0.

Consolation income to all possessors of £1,000 a year ... 0.

(*e*) Income of £2,000 a year; *i.e.*, **x** = 2,000.

2,000 - 1,000 = 1,000.
1,000 squared [*i.e.*, 1,000 multiplied by 1,000] = 1,000,000.

Result of 1,000,000/10,000 = 100.

Income tax paid by all possessors of £2,000 a year ... £100.

Reduced to a tabulated form it becomes evident that the consolation paid by the State to all owners of income below £1,000 will decrease as the incomes increase; until, when a prosperous gentleman attains to £1,000 a year, the consolation will disappear, and instead of *receiving* anything he will begin to *pay* tax upon his income, such tax becoming greater and greater as his income grows—until, if he be so rash as to attain an income of £11,000 a year, he will pay £10,000 a year income tax, and if he does not take this warning and rises to £12,000 a year the State will not only claim all his £12,000 but demand £100 a year more.

That is to say,

A.

Incomes of		
£200	will receive from the State the Consolation of	£64
300	,, ,, ,,	49
400	,, ,, ,,	36
500	,, ,, ,,	25
600	,, ,, ,,	16
700	,, ,, ,,	9
800	,, ,, ,,	4
900	,, ,, ,,	1
1,000	,, ,, ,,	Nil

B.

Incomes of		
£2,000	will pay to the State a Tax of	£100
3,000	,, ,, ,,	400
4,000	,, ,, ,,	900
5,000	,, ,, ,,	1,600
6,000	,, ,, ,,	2,500
7,000	,, ,, ,,	3,600
8,000	,, ,, ,,	4,900
9,000	,, ,, ,,	6,400
10,000	,, ,, ,,	8,100
11,000	,, ,, ,,	10,000
12,000	,, ,, ,,	12,100

*   *   *   *   *

The richest man in the community will thus be he who has an income of £6,000 a year; on this he will have to pay £2,500 income tax, leaving him with an available balance of £3,500 a year to spend! Now was not this anonymous Frenchman a man of real genius? And is he not a signal example of the truth that

"The world knows nothing of its greatest men"?

*   *   *   *   *

The assumptions on which this lofty attempt to reconstruct the social fabric are based are obvious. They are these:—

I. That the earners of daily or weekly wages are not owners of property, nor can they be classed among the possessors of a secure annual income. *De minimis non curat lex.*

II. That it is to the advantage of the community to *increase* the number of small capitalists, and to assist them with State aid—though in a diminishing ratio as their property or incomes increase, and they need less and less encouragement.

III. That it is equally for the advantage of the community to *decrease* the number of large capitalists and to discourage the accumulation of wealth in few hands; and therefore it is necessary to fix a limit of wealth which men shall not be permitted to exceed.

Oh! ye Astors and Vanderbilts! Ye Rothschilds and Barings! Ye kings of railroads and bacon and nitre! Aye! and such as thou citizen Labouchere—thou of the morbidly sensitive conscience. Tremble, for your day is coming! The age of haphazard and empirical finance is passing—the age of scientific and philosophic readjustment is about to dawn. There are those whose mission it will be to set all things straight, and to bring peace on earth and goodwill to men by the exquisitely simple machinery of Fiscal Reform. When that time comes Mammon's Kingdom will sink to be a mere tributary to the great pantisocracy of the future. Hoarding and accumulating will pass away and die—brought to an end by the phlebotomy of the scientists. Money-grubbing will be an incident in the historic romances of that happy time, and the tutored youth, young men and maidens, will smile at the darkness and fumbling stupidity of those untaught generations who only chattered of a golden age, with never a dream that a better age than that would come with the revolving years—to wit, the age of—

$$\cdot 0001\ (\mathbf{x\text{-}m})^2.$$

VII.
WHY I WISH TO VISIT AMERICA.

MANY more years than I like to acknowledge, have passed away since a day when my father caught me slinking out of his library with Mrs. Trollope's "Travels in the United States" under my arm. He laughed at my absurd precocity, for I was little more than a child, and as he took the book away from me, he said, "My boy, that is not a book for you to read. It is not even true. You shall go to America yourself one day, when you're a man, and you'll know better than to write that kind of stuff." It was a great hope that was stirred by that promise that I should go to America myself some day. I used to think about it, and wonder when I might look forward to being a man, and how it could be managed, and who would help me, and whether I should settle there and own a slave. A hundred times I have dreamt of Boston, and of Richmond, for somehow I never thought of New York, and there was no Chicago then, and no San Francisco. Perhaps, too, the United States might collapse before I ever grew to be a man, and that was a prospect that made my heart sick to think of. I have been told, indeed, that one night I awoke with a cry, and was heard to exclaim, "Pray, God, keep America till I've been and seen it!"

And yet I never have seen America, and I am afraid I never shall see it now, though my youthful prayer has been answered, and America has been kept and seems in small danger of collapsing yet awhile. I have read a great many books about America since those days; but I am bound to say they have not made me much in love with the writers, and I am also bound to say that they have given me very, very little information upon exactly those points that I most wished to inquire into. Of late years I have altogether given up this kind of literature. I believe the last time I looked into any one of these so-called "Travels," or "Tours," or "Reminiscences," was when Mr. Anthony Trollope's volumes appeared, and I could not get through them. Somehow my father's words on the mother's book seemed to apply to the son's, and spite of myself his voice seemed to be saying to me, "It is not even true!"

But though I have ceased to read books about America, the strong desire to see the New World has never faded; nay, it has increased in intensity as the years have gone on, and what was at first but a vague hankering after something merely visionary, has gradually become a definite longing to see and know an attainable reality. My friends laugh at me and assure me I should be very much disappointed; that I should not like it; that no man ought to go to the States after thirty; that at Cincinnati there are only hogs to see, and at Chicago only monstrous corn warehouses, at New York only monster hotels, and at Boston—oh, dear! such arrogant prigs; finally, that it would be quite impossible for me to continue wearing a white cravat over there, for the washing of my linen would simply ruin me. I hold my peace, but I am not convinced, and I still wish to visit America. And why is this wish so strong in me? I will try to answer that question as briefly as I can, but I must needs answer it in a disorderly kind of way, and give my reasons as they occur to me, without any attempt at systematic arrangement.

First and foremost, let it be understood that I wish to visit America because I am so very ignorant about the real life of a great nation that has sprung into magnificent maturity in a single century. History has nothing like a parallel to produce, which can for a moment be compared with the growth of this nationality. I use that word advisedly. As to the mere progress in wealth and numbers, that does not impress me much. From anything I have heard or read, it does not seem to me inconceivable that a horde of Chinamen, urged on by avarice and selfishness, might have done quite as much as has been done in the United States in the same time, if John Chinaman had happened to get the start; but if they had done so, they would, I am convinced, have remained a horde of Chinamen still. There would have been no new nation; there would have been nothing like the sublime patriotism that, to my mind, characterizes the great American nation; none of that incomparable chivalry that animated a whole people during the war of secession; none of that proud sensitiveness that surprises cosmopolitan philosophers when they hear Americans speak of "the flag." This is what I should like to look into, like to ask about, like to study on the spot, namely, What is the amazing cohesive force so infinitely potent to bind together into one corporate, living nationality, atoms so dissimilar as the population that makes up the great American people; which, as I understand it does, seems to give a new focus to whatever old love of home warms the breast of German, or Dane, or Swiss, or Englishman; which makes them, one and all, forget their old country and their father's house, and lose all desire to return; which, extinguishing the old love of fatherland, replaces it by a new love, a passion for the glory of the present, with its boundless hopes and ambitions, and an almost haughty contempt for traditions; this exulting confidence in a great destiny which disdains the lessons of experience, and does not ask from them guidance or instruction or warning? Am I wrong? or is it not the fact that Americans have incomparably more faith in the *solvitur ambulando* principle than in any other, and that, whenever it is a question between looking back to see what others have done, and looking forward regardless of all precedent, they always prefer striking out a new line rather than following another's lead? Above all men upon earth, Americans are self-reliant, self-asserting. Yet, was there ever a people so much at unity with itself? Selfishness never seems to diminish the intense national pride; the fierce war of parties in politics never seems to affect patriotism. A whisper of disrespect to "our country," or the semblance of a sneer at it, and woe to you! Is not this so? I should like to see the working of this mysterious and, to my mind, awful force, a force that acts upon the new-comer with exceeding rapidity. How soon does the immigrant feel its operation? By what processes does it exercise its prodigious sway? How is it that the Dutchman, who has spent all his life in Java, looks to lay his bones with his father's at Amsterdam or the Hague; that our own Australian colonists, when they have "made their pile," come back to us and call England still their home; that the Frenchman is always a Frenchman, with an astonishing faculty of producing a bad copy of French fashions wherever he settles, and no power of assimilating himself to the manners and customs of the people among whom he sojourns; but that, when people go to America, it is only a question of time when they will become Americans—become absorbed, that is, into a new nationality? These are questions I should like to ask on the spot, and, if possible, test the truth of the answers suggested.

As there are these problems that present themselves in what I may call the national life of America, so there are others in the political life of the American people that I have never been fortunate enough to find discussed adequately.

We in England have been spending fifty years in timidly feeling our way toward giving our masses a voice in the election of members of Parliament. We are on the eve of a great change, when something very like manhood suffrage will be ushered in among us. It is undeniable that among the upper and middle classes there is a feeling of great uneasiness at the prospect, amounting in some quarters to absolute terror and despair, of what may be coming in the not very distant future. Yet America has prospered in spite of universal suffrage, and, as far as I know, seems to be by no means afraid of it. One hears, indeed, of numbers of dainty people, who are sometimes spoken of as "the upper classes" in American society, affecting to hold aloof from political life and taking no part in the strife of parties. It may be so; but do not these citizens of the great commonwealth who give themselves such airs—these ἄχρηστοι πολῖται, as somebody calls them, who, like naughty children, won't play because they can't always be on the in side—constitute a very insignificant number? The fact remains that the enormous majority of Americans are not only earnest and, if I am rightly informed, passionate politicians, but they go to the polls in shoals. That fact alone strikes some of us here with wonder; and the wonder increases upon us enormously when we are assured that this deep interest in political questions appears to be wholly distinct from the political excitement that intermittently rouses the masses in Europe to outbreaks of frenzied hate against established institutions. In France men get wild with panic lest the *ouvriers* should turn upon the *bourgeoisie*. In Germany the socialists have their own ends in view, and do not disguise them. In Ireland the wretched peasantry avow their designs to confiscate the land. The war of politics with us is eminently selfish, and in proportion as it is carried on with more and more passion the less there seems to be of real patriotism. On our side of the Atlantic it is becoming increasingly apparent that the characteristic of our political warfare may be described as

Each man lusting for all that is not his own.

Mr. Lowell has summed it all up in one of those stinging antitheses that are so stinging they can hardly be true, when, speaking from the American point of view, he says:

Their people's turned to mob—our mob's turned people.

How is it that in America the masses can be disciplined so readily to take their side, and to engage so heartily in the fray, moving together as mysteriously as the swallows that with scarce audible twitterings gather in thousands, plume their

- 160 -

wings for flight, seem to hesitate for a brief hour, and the next are gone? We, indeed, have of late been aping some American practices, and trying our hands at the caucus, and the three hundred, and what not. I suspect it is a very feeble imitation, and I suspect that one of my American friends was right when he said with a laugh: "Your fellows don't know their business; they don't understand what they are talking about. They're first-rate at turning out steel pens and such small ware, but they'd better leave our political machinery alone. You're too crowded up in your little island to find room for one of our big fly-wheels!" But how is all this enthusiasm for politics kept up with comparatively so little appeal to the lowest selfishness? and how are these immense numbers manipulated, the vast armies handled as skilfully as if they were soldiers on parade? It is all inexplicable to large numbers of wiseacres in England, who will persist in talking of petty "motives" and "reason" as if *they* were the prime factors in every social problem.

And this leads me to touch upon another matter, on which I feel myself profoundly ignorant, and which I am sure that others here are quite as ignorant about as I am. We are told that in America there is a recognized profession of politics, just as here there is a medical profession or a legal profession, or, if this is putting the case too strongly, just as here there is the profession of journalism. How in the world do the members of this profession get along? A new President is elected, and we are told that all the old officials are turned out. Where do they go? What becomes of them? What is the effect upon the executive? With us the patronage of the government, at any rate in the civil service, has been reduced to a minimum. Our executive is to a very great extent, indeed, independent of the government of the day. "Men may come and men may go," but permanent secretaries "go on for ever." So do commissioners and their clerks, and the thousands of stipendiaries to whom it matters not one straw whether the Radicals are in or the Tories. With us, when a man has gained an appointment by passing a good examination at eighteen or nineteen years old, it is his own fault if he ever loses it. Practically, there is no getting rid of him as long as he can do his work; he is as safe as a judge, and irremovable. But in America, we hear, every four years they shuffle the cards, and away they go! What results from this? Am I wrongly informed? or is there more absolute patronage, patronage *pur et simple*, in the hands of the President of the United States than in any other hands on the face of the earth? Assuming that it is so, what, I ask, must be the effect upon the moral sentiments of the people at large, inevitably brought day by day and hour by hour into relations with a class of eager office-seekers, hungry, alert, jealous, disappointed, unprincipled, or vindictive, according to their success or failure, in getting what they consider their due. Do the "outs" accept the logic of facts without demur, and forthwith betake themselves to other callings?

That in every change in the chief magistracy of a nation every stipendiary of the executive, from the postman to the judge of the supreme court, should get his dismissal, and the Democrat clerk in the custom-house who was behindhand with his work on Monday evening should leave his arrears to be made up by his Republican successor on Tuesday morning; that when President A enters upon his office, a new game should be begun, and the pieces be all set up again, regardless of the position in which the knights or the pawns were when President B was checkmated,—all this seems to us, from our point of view, not only difficult to understand, but difficult to imagine. Surely, theory and fact in this matter must differ very widely. Am I only exposing my ignorance?

I have used the terms "upper and middle classes" on a previous page. When I have asked Americans what the subtle barriers are that in American society separate class from class, they have replied more than once, "In America there are no classes! We have no differences of rank with us." Strange! And yet we hear of colonels and generals and senators often enough, and I am much mistaken if such titles are at all less esteemed on that side of the water than on this. Be it as it may, however, rank and title may be shadows, but class differences are substantial things. With us the titular aristocracy constitute a class, an inner circle, that at one time united in itself shadow and substance, and now tends to become less exclusive and less influential, however loudly some may complain that

... in these British islands 'Tis the substance that wanes ever, 'tis the symbol that exceeds.

We love rank, because we have a lingering suspicion that it somehow symbolizes wealth, or power, or brilliant intellectual gifts, or great public services, that have forced their possessors into the front rank at some time or other, and received their due recognition in the shape of titular distinction conferred either recently or in days gone by. But if a title is found to be dissociated from any nobleness of character, and is unsupported by brain power or purse power, it will not save a man from humiliating snubs, or give him the *entrée* to the drawing-rooms of the upper classes. For we have more than one upper class among us, as other nations have had and will continue to have while the world lasts. In that social world where Mrs. Grundy bears sway, our titular aristocracy undoubtedly are the acknowledged leaders, and to them great homage is paid. But it is not only because a man is an earl, or a lady is a duchess, that the one or the other is surrounded by a little court, approached with deference and treated with studied respect, but because both the one and the other are rich enough to "support the title," as we say. Yes, it is true that in some sense or other

Our nobles wear their ermine on the outside, or walk blacklyIn presence of the social law, as most ignoble men.

You may protest that society in England is under the dominion of a plutocracy, then. Yes! and No! Yes! in so far as it is true and always must be true, that no man or woman can live on familiar terms, and keep up the habitual intercourse with the leisure classes, without a certain amount of money. No! in so far as it is also true that money alone, however abundant it may be, will never, among us, give any one an introduction to what we call society. I have heard of cases, and I know of one, where a millionaire from our colonies took a palace in London, and lived *en prince*; was visited by no one, failed to get into any but a third-rate club, found no one to entertain and but few people to speak to; and finally has gone back from whence he came, astonished, disappointed, and soured. They tell me that wealth in America will gain admission to any society for any one. I have been repeatedly assured by intelligent Americans that this is so; yet I cannot understand that it should be so. I can quite understand that, whatever a man's rank, or gifts, or prospects may be, he would find it very painful to mix with the upper ten thousand if he could not afford to pay for cab-hire, or keep up his subscription at the club, every day finding it hard to get his dinner, and every night perplexed *de lodice paranda*; but I can no more understand how a mere expenditure of cash could get X, Y, or Z into the best society, than I can understand how a payment of, say £10,000, would get an average cricketer into the All-England eleven, or a second-rate oar into the University crew. The Corporation of London is a plutocracy; but society, while accepting his lavish hospitality, treats even the Lord Mayor of London *de haut en bas*. The Lady Mayoress receives ambassadors with condescension; next year some young *attaché* stares at Mrs. Tomkins, and wonders where he has met that woman.

Who are the upper classes in America? It is nonsense to say there are none. Not to speak of those states in pre-Christian times that tended more or less to become dominated over by an oligarchy, Athens was at least as pure a republic as America is; her people were as proud, as self-asserting, as audaciously enterprising, as ambitious, as shrewd in commercial ventures, as greedy for money, and as lavish in spending it, as the Americans are; yet the "first families" among the Athenians were as haughty as Spaniards, as exclusive as the old French noblesse, and bragged of their ancestry as absurdly as Scotchmen do. If a loud-voiced, bawling demagogue came to the front by sheer force of will and impudence, his political opponents never allowed the populace to forget that he was brought up in a tan-yard. Demosthenes gives point to his most withering sarcasms against Æschines by reminding his audience that he was the son of a school-mistress, and had to scrub the ink off the desks at which his mother taught the dirty little urchins; and who that has read the "Clouds" can forget Strepsiades's doleful lamentation over his fatal mistake in marrying a fine lady with a pedigree, and begetting a son who did not take after his father? There must be an aristocracy in America who stand upon their birth rather than their mere wealth, yet how little we hear of them. What recognition do they receive? How is it they so seldom come to be leaders? How is it that Hyperbolus seems to push aside Cimon, and Cleon is quite too much for Alcibiades?

It used to be said that no two Englishmen could be found to maintain a conversation together for five minutes without one asking the other what he thought of the weather. It is true still; but there is another question that of late years has become the stock question when two people meet one another, and that is, "When are you going away?" If a man replies boldly that he is not going away at all, he is looked upon as the very impersonation of eccentricity. "Not going away! Why, what are you going to do?" This "going away" means leaving our country-houses when the flowers are in their splendour and all nature bids us stay where we are, and starting off for Norway or Switzerland to spend our money among strange people, drink bad wine, get in late for *table-d'hôte* when we are faint and weary, or find ourselves five flights of stairs from our pocket handkerchief in a towering edifice without a lift. But go where we will, we are sure to find ourselves not two chairs away from American tourists; they are everywhere. Sir James Ross used to say that if ever he reached the North Pole he would be sure to find a Scotchman sitting upon it. I don't know what has become of all the Scotchmen; they and the gypsies have grown rarer since I was a boy; but you can never escape from Americans. Of course there are Americans and Americans; they differ from one another as much as any other people do, as much and no more; but this is true of all the transatlantic tourists, they are abundantly supplied with money, and they do not grudge spending it; in fact, if we were to judge by the Americans we meet with in Europe, we should be forced to the conclusion that all Americans are rich, even very rich. But when I have asked them how clergymen and doctors and lawyers and elderly people with strictly limited incomes live in the United States,—such people as among us live in comfort with a couple of female servants, or even keep a pony chaise,— I have found my tourist acquaintances very much amused at my supposing that in America *helps* could be got to stay in such a household. "Are there, then, no small people in America?" I have asked. The answer has been more often than not, "If there are, we don't know them."

It is obvious that quiet, domestic people of small means are not to be met with among tourists at luxurious hotels, and equally obvious that such people are hard to get at by travellers who are themselves birds of passage. When a householder is living very near the wind, he does not like to expose his small economies and humble ways to a stranger; and because he is living a quiet, unostentatious life, he has little to offer to those whose occupation is seeing sights. But any man or woman who wishes to gain some insight into our domestic life may easily obtain it if he will but take the trouble to read our works of fiction. Our novelists come from the middle classes, not from the rich or leisure classes, and they speak as they do know. They tell us all about the habits and sentiments and ways of talking among clergymen and doctors and farmers and millers and clerks and shopkeepers in England; they show us the good and the bad side with equal impartiality; and no more faithful delineations have ever been made of the inner and outer life of the lowest struggling classes than are to be found in English literature. But if we want to get an insight into the *morale* of such people in America, we do not know where to look for it. Such a character as Kitty Ellison in Mr. Howell's "Chance Aquaintance," whose heart is with Uncle Jack and his anxieties and troubles while she is enjoying all the gaieties and luxuries that wealth can bestow, is a rarity in America; and, moreover, all the people one meets with in Mr. Howell's stories are away from home. In the "Biglow Papers" one does now and then get a hint that there are shrewd farmers and hard-headed country folk somewhere in the States, who do not wander very far, but one never gets to know them. That exquisite story of Mr. Stockton's, "Rudder Grange," as far as I know, occupies a unique position in American literature, and has for many of us lifted the veil from a whole world of little people across the Atlantic, of whose very existence some on our side the water had almost begun to entertain doubts. Yet we are in the habit of thinking that it is precisely among these people that we must look for the real heart of a great nation, and that the pulse of every great nation is to be felt among them, if at all.

But of all subjects of inquiry that a thoughtful Englishman could set himself to work at, the most instructive, the most suggestive, would be the effect of perfect equality between the various religious bodies upon the philosophic speculations, religious sentiments, and ethical convictions of the American people. In England there is one Church by law established, and they who separate from the communion of that Church are all classed together as dissenters. That there should be anywhere on the face of the earth a condition of society where there can be no such thing as a dissenter, is a thought extremely difficult for some good folks here to grasp. But much harder is the other notion, which I presume is familiar enough to Americans, that there should be anywhere no sects. No dissenters, because no predominant or paramount Christian organization that rejoices in the "most-favoured-nation" clause. No sects, because no church recognized as *the* Church from which the other religious bodies have cut themselves off. That there should be no bigotry and exclusiveness, no *odium theologicum*, no fierce rivalry, no proselytizing, in America, as everywhere else, is inconceivable. Theological disputants will cease to wrangle when lawyers learn to love one another as brethren and doctors differ without asperity; but among us the situation is extremely embarrassing as between the Church— for with us it is *the* Church—and the non-conformist, that is, with those who will not subscribe to our Church doctrine, accept our formularies, or conform to our liturgy. Here we have a standard by which we try all other Christian bodies, and we pronounce them more or less orthodox or denounce them as absolutely unorthodox, in proportion as they approach or depart from this standard which is tacitly accepted among us as the established standard. If there were no Church of England by law established, I believe that a vast number of people would find themselves quite dazed, quite lost. To them it would be practically pretty much as if we were all to awake some fine morning to find that the Home Secretary had shut up Greenwich observatory and run away with the key, having previously taken measures to stop all the great clocks in the land. We should all of us be going by our own watches.

Yet somehow in America every man goes by his own watch; and if nobody is right, nobody else is likely to consider himself hopelessly wrong. Here the social position of the clergy of the established Church is something quite peculiar. There is no need to dwell upon the fact, but that it is a fact there can be no doubt. The result is, that the attitude of the clergy9 toward all the religious teachers has always been exclusive; there has never been any cordiality, and very little coöperation. I do not say this is not deplorable; I am concerned with facts only. A supercilious tone is so habitually natural to the clergyman when speaking or dealing with the dissenting minister, and a tone of soreness, jealousy, and suspicion on the part of the minister towards the clergyman seems to us so inseparable from their relations one to the other, that we in England can hardly bring ourselves to believe that the Episcopalian and the Independent, the Wesleyan and the Primitive Methodist, could meet on absolutely equal terms, just as officers of two regiments in the same army can meet at mess and fight valiantly side by side against the common foe. Every now and then we get one of those necessary evils, the religious newspapers, sent us by kind friends from America, or we catch a glimpse of an American bishop or Episcopalian popular preacher. Was it only a dream, or have I really, actually, in the flesh, once met with an American archdeacon? But from these exalted personages and their organs surprisingly little is to be learned; and I observe that an ecclesiastic, let him come from where he

- 167 -

may, is a shy creature, ready enough to listen, but not to talk. He puts himself on the defensive, and is so very much afraid of committing himself, that you are apt to retire into your interior, too; just as I have observed two snails meeting on their evening walk; one at the approach of his brother shuts himself up in his shell, and the other tickles at him with his horns for a little while, but ends by accepting the situation, and shutting himself up also. Result, to all appearance, nothing but two unoccupied snail-shells, inhabitants having retired from publicity.

I cannot believe that even in America the priests of the Roman Church would ever assume any other than a haughty bearing toward all other Christian teachers. Theirs is either *the* Church, or it is nothing. But how do all the rest behave to one another? Are they all, in point of fact, merely ministers of their respective congregations? How about proselytizing? It is comparatively easy to draw up a constitution that shall keep up a certain amount of discipline among the officers of any force; but it is quite another thing to keep control over the rank and file when they are all volunteers. Such a regiment as that famous one of Artemus Ward's, "composed exclusively of commanders-in-chief," would hardly be found a successful organization in the church militant. Are the clergy of all denominations held by all denominations in equal esteem? Do they "love as brethren," or do they "bite and devour one another?"

*   *   *   *   *

These are some of the questions I find myself continually asking when I turn my thoughts toward the magnificent country and the great nation on the other side of the ocean. I do not believe a man could get any answer to them, satisfactory to his own mind, except by personal observation. He must for a time live among living men, and see them at their daily tasks, to understand their life even a very little. It is too much the habit of travellers to take their theories with them. I, for my part, have none. If I ever carry out the wish of my life, I shall start as a naturalist does who goes to make collections—with empty cases, notebooks, and apparatus—not too ready to generalize, but very anxious to learn. The probability is, I shall never go at all. But others more fortunate than I may, perhaps, be able to enlighten my darkness and inform my ignorance, and it may happen that the hints I have thrown out may be suggestive to them.

As to the big cities, with their colossal warehouses and enormous trade, their gigantic hotels and prodigious growth, they possess for me no attraction. There is something dreadful to my mind in losing my personality in a surging multitude and being absorbed in a crowd. To find myself unable to hear my own voice because steam-hammers are pounding all round me, and iron wheels are keeping up a ceaseless din, annihilating articulate speech—that seems to me horrible. I shrink from these things. I should be found creeping into out-of-the-way places, prying into schools and colleges and universities, begging that nobody would notice me, while I might be permitted to notice everybody. Sometimes I should put very impertinent questions about the wonderful endowments that I hear Americans believe in firmly, just when we are beginning to lose our faith in their value. Sometimes I should even venture to inquire about the war—*the* war—the one war that reflected only imperishable glory upon both sides—the one civil war in the world's history that ended with the grandest of all triumphs, freedom to the oppressed, without one single act of vengeance inflicted upon the beaten side. Sometimes—but I am in danger of treading upon perilous ground, in danger of saying too much, in danger of making some one growl out suspiciously, "When you do come, if ever you do, you'd better keep out of my way!"

*   *   *   *   *

A few days ago, I was turning over an old volume of "Punch," when I was attracted by a cartoon that may be familiar to some of my readers. A mighty coal-heaver, his day's work done, is leaning against one of the many posts to be found in the region of the Seven Dials, his hands in his pockets, his lips pipeless, his eyes staring at vacancy. By him stands an exquisitely dressed clergyman, tall, slim, gentle, refined, who has blandly laid his extended hand upon the other's brawny shoulder. Says the clergyman, "My friend, I want to go to Exeter Hall." Says the coal-heaver, "Then why the dooce don't you go?" Was it that the good man did not know his way? or was he suffering from a little tightness in the chest?

FOOTNOTES

1 "Arcady, for Better for Worse."

2 This is a matter of very great importance in hundreds of country parishes, where the washing of the rectory frequently suffices to maintain a whole family.

3 A genuine Norfolk man never aspirates a *t* when followed by an *r*. It is always *trew* for through, *troat* for throat, *tree* for three, &c.

4 I do not forget Crabbe—that sweet and gentle versifier. But the romantic element is wholly wanting in him. Very probably Sir Wilfrid Lawson would vehemently protest that Crabbe deserves to be reckoned among the greatest of the great. Was not his first poem entitled *Inebriety*? When a child I used to be told that Bloomfield's *Farmer's Boy* was equal to Spenser, but I concluded that Spenser must be very dull, and conceived a horror of the *Faery Queen* in consequence.

5 The lists of "church goods"—*i.e.* of the contents of our churches—during the reign of Edward the Sixth, are to be found in the Record Office. Many of them have been printed *in extenso*; they make up in the aggregate a large mass of documents, and some account of them may be found in the seventh and ninth reports of the Deputy Keeper of the Public Records. Among the miscellaneous books of the Exchequer is a visitation book of the Archdeacon of Norwich for the year 1368, which contains a very minute account of the contents of every church in the archdeaconry, including service books, vestments, sacred vessels, banners, processional crosses, ornaments, &c., all set down in detail, the names of the donors being frequently given, and sometimes the value of the more precious articles being stated. Some years ago I stumbled upon an inventory of the contents of the Collegiate Church of St. Mary, Warwick, drawn up in 1467, extending over five folio pages. It seemed to me, on a cursory inspection, to be a document of great value as illustrative of this subject. I know not whether it has ever been printed; if not, perhaps Warwickshire antiquaries may be glad to be referred to it— *Miscell. Books of the Exchequer*, Q.R. No. 30. The inventory begins at fol. cci.

6 Why *will* not the printers' readers let me use this word? I *do* use it every day of my life in talk; why may I not write it and print it? It is very short, and it is perfectly harmless. I am afraid it must mean something bad in Finnish or some other strange tongue, for the *reader* always draws my attention to it.

7 Fact! Old Biddy's habit of *dashing it* is so confirmed that there's no hope of her outgrowing it.

8 Inasmuch as the *general reader* has a strong objection to the use of Decimals, it will be a comfort to him to be assured that *multiplying* by ·0001 is the same thing as *dividing* by 10,000; and so ·0001 $(\mathbf{x} - \mathbf{m})^2$ is only another way of writing $((\mathbf{x} - \mathbf{m})^2)/10,000$

9 It has been only of late years that any Christian ministers other than those ordained by the bishops of the Church of England have been called "clergymen" among us. The nonconformists were always called "ministers" or "preachers." I find myself driven to use the words "clergy" and "minister" in the old way, to avoid conveying a wrong impression to my readers.

Milton Keynes UK
Ingram Content Group UK Ltd.
UKHW030740071024
449371UK00006B/677

9 789362 095992